Beyond Fear

TWELVE SP[...]
TO RACIA[...]

Aeeshah Ababio Clottey
and
Kokomon Clottey

H J KRAMER
TIBURON, CALIFORNIA

The symbol on the cover is one version of the Sankofa bird, an ancient Adinkra symbol from the Akan Tribe of Ghana, West Africa. The Sankofa bird retrieves its past, cleansing it as it moves forward in time; it represents the wisdom of learning from the past, retaining only the healing and love so one can live more fully in the present and create a brighter future.

H J Kramer Inc
P.O. Box 1082
Tiburon, CA 94920

Editor: Nancy Grimley Carleton
Editorial Assistants: Claudette Charbonneau and Emily Acker
Cover Design: Jim Marin/Marin Graphic Services
Composition: Classic Typography
Manufactured in the United States of America.
10 9 8 7 6 5 4 3 2 1

Library of Congress Cataloging-in-Publication Data

Clottey, Aeeshah Ababio, 1949–
    Beyond fear : twelve spiritual keys to racial healing / Aeeshah
Ababio-Clottey and Kokomon Clottey.
       p.   cm.
    Includes bibliographical references.
    ISBN 0-915811-82-0 (alk. paper)
    1. Racism—United States—Psychological aspects. 2. United
States—Race relations—Psychological aspects. 3. Mental healing.
4. Attitude (Psychology). 5. Conduct of life. I. Clottey, Kokomon,
1949– . II. Title.
E185.615.C633 1999
305.8'00973—DC21   98-20399
                                  CIP

We humbly dedicate this book to the millions of Africans who died in the middle passage, to the 6 million Jews who died in the European Holocaust, to the millions of Native Americans killed during the opening of the West, and to the millions who died in needless wars. This is but a token of what you deserve. We ask for your forgiveness, for we have met the enemy in us.

We are writing this book because it is our own desire to be whole, healed human beings who are in touch with our reason for being here and our purpose in life here on earth—and our primary purpose is to share love.

AEESHAH ABABIO CLOTTEY and KOKOMON CLOTTEY

To Our Readers

The books we publish
are our contribution to an
emerging world based on cooperation
rather than on competition, on affirmation
of the human spirit rather than on self-doubt,
and on the certainty that all humanity is
connected. Our goal is to touch as many
lives as possible with a message
of hope for a better world.

Hal and Linda Kramer, Publishers

Contents

Foreword

E very Thursday night at the Church of Today in Warren, Michigan, thirty or forty people gather for a Racial Healing group. The group is not easy. It is emotionally messy and psychologically draining. At times I have thought, "Is this really worth it? This conversation might be doing more harm than good."

Yet we all keep coming. There's some sense that we have to do this, some absolute understanding that the only way around this mess is through it. Racial tension exists in America, and to deny it is ridiculous. To heal it takes, to use Aeeshah's expression, "heart work." Heart work isn't easy work, but it is possible and it is necessary.

One night, after one of the Racial Healing groups when I felt particularly dismayed by the process, I began to read Aeeshah and Kokomon's book, *Beyond Fear.* I was so relieved to read their stories, to learn of their transformations, to understand how one could apply the principles of *A Course in Miracles* to this particular wound on our nation's psyche. I knew the principles of attitudinal healing, but it wasn't until I read this book that I could really see through to the possibility that race relations in the United States could move "beyond fear."

I think race is America's most urgent issue. It is a bleeding wound, sometimes on top and sometimes beneath the surface of our civic skin. Every year, more young people give up on the American dream. Every year, the signs of hatred grow more and more foreboding. Every year, fear continues to grow like a cancer among us.

Only love can set us free.

Aeeshah and Kokomon have journeyed to the love that heals the racial heart. I for one am very grateful for their direction. I know what this book has done for me, and for my friends who share with me the vision of an America which has healed itself. If enough of us read this book and practice its principles, then America will have a miracle. As it says in *A Course in Miracles,* "The holiest spot on earth is where an ancient hatred has become a present love."

In that sense, what you hold in your hands is a holy book. Let's take it to our hearts. There is so very, very much at stake.

—Marianne Williamson

Preface

The Hispanic immigrant who became a citizen yesterday must be as precious to us as the Mayflower descendant. It is our diversity that makes us strong. Yet our diversity has sadly through our history also been the source of our discrimination—discrimination that we as guardians of the American dream must rip out, branch and roots.

RETIRED GENERAL COLIN POWELL

The devastating effects of racism confront us with the deepest challenges we as a nation and we as individuals face. Recent events reveal open wounds and ugly scars—from the reactions concerning the O. J. Simpson trial to the aftermath of the Rodney King beating, from the fundraising scandal focusing on donors of Asian descent to the initiatives against affirmative action in California and Texas, and the deep animosity focused against immigrants from Third World countries. It is apparent that our society requires profound racial healing if we are to move beyond fear to claim the promise of our humanity.

Indeed, the racial divisions and excruciating pain of the racism in our midst have become one of the most talked-about subjects in our country today. President Clinton himself has recognized its grave importance, calling racism a curse upon America and declaring a year of national reflection and initiative geared toward healing this malady. From the president to community leaders, we hear much discussion about the importance of building harmony along racial lines. We wonder whether we could all learn "to get along," to use Rodney King's famous plea as he attempted to quell the riots following the Simi Valley verdict. Yet underneath the talk lies an enormous reservoir of hopelessness and fear. This hopelessness and fear have kept us stuck, preventing us from coming up with the creative solutions that lie within our power to implement. The roots of racism in our country precede its founding, and the relationships among America's diverse groups have posed a dilemma at least since the Declaration of Independence.

We are writing this book because we deeply believe that it is time for us to do the personal healing work that will alleviate the malady of racism. With all the hopelessness and tension surrounding this issue, it is well past time for us to find the willingness and the courage to do the work that would help us move to a place of hope and positive intention, a place beyond fear. We believe we bring to this topic a unique perspective. One of us, Aeeshah, is an African American woman whose life led her from the warmth of her family's love in the South, to the empowerment and separation of the Nation of Islam, and finally to the deep personal healing arising from her awakening to the principles of attitudinal healing, which we will be describing in this book. One of us, Kokomon, started his life in Ghana, Africa, framed by the residue of colonialism and tribalism, then faced the poison of racism after his immigration to the United States, going on to find healing, like Aeeshah, through the liberating principles of attitudinal healing. Together, we have directed the Attitudinal Healing Connection in the heart of West Oakland for the past five years. This is where we live and work, having dedicated our lives to healing racism by moving beyond fear.

Preface

As Americans, many of us feel that we could never let go of the specialness that we have inherited from our race-conscious society. We group one another according to shapes, sizes, and colors at such a deep level that it has become automatic. We label and judge one another along racial lines, even when we aren't conscious of what we're doing. We find it very difficult to accept the uniqueness of each individual. We tend to see all blacks the same way, all whites the same way, all Asians the same way, and so on through every racial grouping, even if we aren't aware of it. Before we can find healing on a national or global level, we must each find the way to heal our personal wounding around the issue of race.

This book tells our story as two individuals as we share with you how we began to heal, and how we have come to extend our healing to others. We're thankful that you're joining us as you read this book. We welcome you as you travel with us on this journey—a journey through the heart of racial separation toward the richness and inner peace that await us as we move past old barriers and join together to heal racism at its deepest levels.

—Aeeshah Ababio Clottey and Kokomon Clottey
Oakland, California

Acknowledgments

Our deepest and most abiding gratitude goes to God and our ancestors who came before us.

We are also deeply grateful to the late singer John Denver, who, out of his compassion and reverence for all life, founded Windstar, an organization dedicated to environmental and global healing. In addition, our gratitude is extended to Dr. Gerald (Jerry) Jampolsky and Dr. Diane Cirincione for their recommendation to us to present "Healing the Negative Effects of Racism" at the annual Windstar Symposium in 1995. That experience provided the catalyst for the book you are now reading. At the end of our talk, we met Hal and Linda Kramer, our publishers, who recognized the need for such an important work. Words cannot express the gratitude we feel for their vision and support of this project.

We also wish to extend our heartfelt thanks to Judith S. Whitson and Robert Skutch and the Foundation for Inner Peace for their permission to utilize material from *A Course in Miracles*, which provided the foundation for this book.

Our warm thanks and love go to Nancy Carleton, our editor, for her guidance, support, encouragement, and loving nurturing of this book from conception to completion. We also deeply appreciate the editorial assistance of Claudette Charbonneau and Emily Acker.

We are most thankful to Bob Sandoe, Fahizah Alim, Sandra Snell, Carla Oden-Santiego, Matthew Fox, and Dorothy Presley for their love and support and feedback on early drafts of this book.

Acknowledgments

Our gratitude and love are extended to the following people whose support and love helped us to bring this work to fruition: We thank Amanah Harris for her work with the children at the Attitudinal Healing Connection, Inc., in Oakland, and Dezorah Smith for her wise counsel as the on-site consultant. We are grateful to the Board members who are so supportive of the healing work we facilitate: Nadirah Sharifah Ihsan, Peter Wu, and Debbie West-Wu. Other people and organizations who helped with this work and whose faith, love, and support make our work easier were Lillia Cooksey, Rhea Garboos, Tom Pinkson, Terryl Kistler, Ghanabà, John and Deo Robbins, the Center for Attitudinal Healing in Sausalito, California, the Network for Attitudinal Healing International, and the Wakan Community in San Rafael, California. Our deepest thanks to all!

Introduction

*This is not a time in America to minimize our
antagonisms or pretend they don't exist. This is a
time for serious people to try, with depth of intelligence
and heart, to build new bridges. The most important
reconciliation needed in America today is in the area of
race. With a nation, as with an individual, amends are
necessary to free the psyche and allow it to move on.*

MARIANNE WILLIAMSON,
The Healing of America

Here at the Attitudinal Healing Connection in West Oakland, we define racism as a life-threatening disease. As the death rates of inner city black youth make clear, racism is a life-and-death matter, one which affects each and every one of us, for we are all connected. The problem of racism is intricately related to the problem of separation, of feeling different from and separate from. This is a spiritual dilemma, and as such we are aware of a deep need for a spiritual approach to healing this disease, even more important than governmental legislation. It is up to each of us to make the commitment to break free from the bonds of racism.

Racism may manifest in whites as an inherent or subconscious need to feel superior to blacks or other non-whites. And it may create a sense of inferiority among blacks and other non-whites that inhibits their development and self-empowerment. Racism also has fostered strong feelings of suspicion on the part of black people toward white people. Over the centuries, the pain which black people have experienced makes this suspicion difficult to overcome. Feelings of superiority or inferiority, of suspicion and mistrust, can manifest in the people of any race or ethnic group. They also come into play any time humans define differences between themselves and another group, whether with regard to religion, national origin, sexual orientation, or race—anytime we define a group or person as the "other."

In our work in the United States, we have found that getting white people to acknowledge that they are infected with racism can be difficult. Often they experience deep shame out of the intellectual recognition that racism is bad. The legacy of centuries of oppressive behavior has contaminated thinking and feeling for everyone. No one wants to be associated with a behavior that is almost universally recognized as evil. Many white people of goodwill have repressed their negative feelings about black people and other non-whites. This difficulty in owning up to racist feelings is not unique to white people, however. Acknowledging racist feelings can be very difficult for people of every race. Therefore, each of us must begin to recognize the need to move beyond fear and heal in this area.

A Perspective on Race

The concept of race is a social and cultural construction. . . .
Race simply cannot be tested or proven scientifically.
It is clear that human populations are not unambiguous,
clearly demarcated, biologically distinct groups.
The concept of "race" has no validity . . . in the human species.

THE AMERICAN ANTHROPOLOGICAL ASSOCIATION

Most of us know that on the biological, scientific level, races do not exist. There simply is no clear demarcation between different racial groups of people. Humanity is all one race—the human race. The idea of races is something that humans made up to divide and separate people. A well-respected philosopher and scientist, Carl Von Linne, better known as Linnaeus, originated the current idea of races back in 1735. An eighteenth-century admirer of Linnaeus, Blumenbach, promoted the classification of races with rankings of superiority and inferiority. In other words, the modern notion of race became a defining factor for humanity in the eighteenth century, although racial differentiation has certainly been present for much of human history. In a spiritual sense, the identification of separate races can perhaps be considered part of our fall from grace—as we adopted the concept of separation rather than unity. Although the concept of racial identity is illusory, we have all grown up in cultures that have instilled in us the idea of race from an early age, so we have to deal with it. There is no way to avoid this level of our conditioning. The only way to the other side—where true healing and racial harmony are both possible and present—is to go through the swamp of mistaken ideas and face our preconceptions and our prejudices. All prejudice in a sense is a misguided commitment to our ignorance, a mistaken devotion to our fear and our biases.

In order to work with our biases and move through our ignorance, we need to rediscover some ancient spiritual precepts and work with them. These spiritual truths are present today in contemporary form in the principles of attitudinal healing, which we will be sharing with you in Part Two. These principles teach that it is our deepest desire to be whole, healed human beings who are in touch with our reason for being here and our purpose in life here on earth—and our primary purpose is to share love.

Exercise to Clarify Your Intentions

Exploring ideas and feelings about racism can be difficult. In our work with many people of many different racial backgrounds, we have found that holding a clear intention helps set the most fertile ground for the healing process. The exercises included at the end of each chapter in this book can help you clarify your intentions and participate directly in the process of racial healing. We encourage you to take the time to engage with the steps suggested here and throughout the book.

1. Before you read the rest of this book, consider ways to actively state your intention. Maybe one or more of the following ideas will fit for you.

Intentions as I Read This Book

- As I read this book, I intend to look honestly at my own prejudices and preconceptions so I can heal them.
- I will practice observing my judgments about race and about joining across racial barriers, and I will try to be fully open-minded.
- I will vigilantly monitor my attitudes and acknowledge when I am tempted to name-call or discriminate in any way.
- I intend to move swiftly to choose to heal any attitude that condemns others or that is biased in any way.

- One person can make a difference, and I intend to do my part to bridge the gap between the races by healing my own mind.

- Just being tolerant of differences is not enough; to truly bridge the racial divide, I intend to accept and honor differences.

- My intention is to bring my consciousness to bear whenever I assume that the "other" is not intelligent. I will summon myself to address this attitude immediately.

- Whenever I am faced with a racial conflict, I will endeavor not to blame others, so that I can practice clear communication.

- I will play my part in making equality of opportunity to all a reality.

- I intend to make it my personal mission to heal hate and intolerance, beginning with myself.

PART ONE

Telling Our Stories

Healing Through Storytelling

Hope is a state of mind, not of the world. Either we
have hope within us or we don't; it is a dimension
of the soul, and it's not dependent on some observation
of the world or estimate of the situation.
Hope is not prognostication. It is an orientation
of the spirit, an orientation of the heart; it transcends
the world that is immediately experienced,
and is anchored somewhere beyond its horizons.
Hope, in this deep and powerful sense, is not the same
as joy that things are going well, or willingness to invest in
enterprises that are obviously heading for success,
but rather an ability to work for something because it is good,
not just because it stands a chance to succeed.
Hope is definitely not the same thing as optimism.
It is not the conviction that something will turn out well,
but the certainty that something makes sense,
regardless of how it turns out.

VACLAV HAVEL

Telling Our Stories

Throughout this book, we—Aeeshah and Kokomon—will be sharing our personal stories and experiences. Following the African tradition, we believe that it is through the telling of our stories that we are healed. As we share our stories with you, we take our own personal healing to a deeper place. The process of storytelling is a gift that we've been given to complete our own personal healing process. Writing our stories represents a new beginning for us, but as you read them you will see that we have been doing the heart work of healing for a long time. Healing is a lifelong process of learning to let go of the fear, anger, shame, guilt, and victimization from our own past so we can experience our present relationships more fully.

By looking at our past, at our history, we come to know our preconceptions, the underlying judgments that form the basis for prejudice. We learn to look at these preconceptions with compassion rather than judgment. As we do this, we explore the core of how we're all joined and connected, the oneness of humanity. Of course, we're doing this for ourselves—for our personal healing—but we're also doing this for our children. Both Native American traditions and African traditions state that any work or healing that you do for yourself, you are also doing for the next seven generations to come—for your children and your children's children. It is the belief of Kokomon's people, the Ga Tribe in Ghana, West Africa, that when a family member passes on, what is known as "Home-Going" does not end that individual's membership in the tribe or family. With the strong emphasis in Africa on ancestors, it is also understood that in doing the work of personal healing, you are also doing the work for the seven generations that came before you—for your grandparents, and your great grandparents, and your great great grandparents, and so on. You're not just doing it for you.

As you undertake the journey of racial healing, be aware that you may experience some intense emotions. You may encounter internal resistance as you read certain parts of our stories and as you begin to tell your own story. Do not allow the fear of looking within to stop our journey together, for you are not journeying for yourself alone. We offer the following suggestions as pillows to support you on your journey:

1. Take your time and read the book slowly, over a period of weeks, not days.
2. Allow yourself to absorb each chapter before moving on.
3. Work with the ideas presented as objectively as you can; begin to tell your own story as honestly as you can.
4. Remember that this book is about joining, not separation. So, as you journey with us, let kindness be your constant companion.

We are never healed alone. We want to emphasize again that whenever you heal yourself, you are healing your family, your local community, and ultimately the world we all share. When we share our stories, we unfold the divinity within us, and share it with one another.

We encourage all of our readers to get in the habit of telling their stories. In the groups for healing racism that we facilitate, storytelling by the group members is one of the most important tools for transformation. We tell our stories without judgment or condemnation, and we listen to one another's stories with compassion and acceptance. It's helpful to have a real live human being to tell your story to, but even as you read this book you can start the process by telling your story to yourself. In this way, you can begin the journey toward racial healing. Later, in Chapter 16, we'll suggest how you can continue this process by setting up your own Healing Racism Circle.

CHAPTER ONE

Early Messages

Dolphins tell us with their eyes
What soul within should realize,
That intellect and reasoning
May only bring a reckoning.
We must embrace the cosmic mind
And not enslave another kind.
We must embrace the cosmic heart
To loose the ties that keep us part.

ROLLAND G. SMITH

We (Aeeshah and Kokomon) come from very different backgrounds, but as we began to unfold our stories together, we learned that prejudice and intolerance are not confined to the United States. Kokomon's experiences with colonialism and tribalism growing up in Ghana revealed their deep roots in prejudice and intolerance, just as Aeeshah faced the effects of racism growing up in the Deep South of the United States of America. As we write about our lives, we hope you will also reflect on your own life, and the messages you received and internalized about race as a child.

Aeeshah's Childhood

I grew up in Louisiana, a state whose race relations were among the poorest in the United States, but the love of my family buffered me from some of the most debilitating effects of racial discrimination. I was the youngest of twelve children born to Robert and Gussie Persley in a county hospital in Shreveport, Louisiana, and we lived in the family home in a small town about forty-five miles south of Shreveport.

My mother began her career as a beautician in 1949, the year I was born. I remember spending a lot of time in my mother's beauty shop, listening to the women talk. In her own way, my mother was a natural psychologist and social worker. Sometimes I thought that few but licensed therapists receiving an hourly fee could bear to listen to the stories my mother heard daily from those women. She gave them her undivided attention, as well as positive suggestions on how they could resolve their life issues.

The beauty shop was my first school, and I learned from my mother as well as my older sisters, who gave me instructions in daily skills, such as cooking, cleaning house, and sewing. Our family was like a complete community within itself. Much of our food came out of our garden, and my father and two brothers shared in the household chores.

Following the tradition of Abraham Lincoln, my mother was a Republican. She was also a strong Christian who was very proud of her heritage. We grew up going to church and serving God. My father, however, had little patience with church, and he often complained that the ministers were all crooks, just out to get his hard-earned money. He felt that a man should do practical work to earn a living.

My mother was of mixed race, a tall woman with light brown skin, and she was considered to be very beautiful. She told us of her Apache and Caucasian heritage and said that her temperament came from the Apache blood that flowed through her veins. She talked less about her African heritage, but she shared with us about the important role black people had played in building this country. My parents met while my father was visiting in Jefferson, Texas. The two fell in love, and they moved to his family hometown in Stonewall, Louisiana.

My father came from a very large family. In those days, they were considered well-off because they were among the few black landowners in Stonewall. My father's family wasn't very open to my mother. According to my mother, they rejected her because of her fair skin. My father's people were very black people—almost pure African with a trace of Cherokee blood. Even among black people, the color line served as a measuring stick. We as blacks have internalized the racist beliefs of our society. Often if you were lighter in skin tone, you would be treated with more respect, even among black people. However, my father's sisters decided as soon as they saw my mother that she was not going to have a place above them.

I remember we moved to Coushatta when I was about four years old. My father had finally purchased his own home. He left the family home to keep peace in his marriage with my mother. Coushatta would be my hometown until I was seventeen.

Both my parents had a strong work ethic and believed in "doing for oneself." Back in those days, only the poor whites in our small town could receive government stipends. Black people were able to receive some government food items, but my mother forbade us to eat government food.

As I reflect on some of the early incidents in my life that made me aware of racial differences, I remember a time when we went on our annual Fourth of July barbecue. I was about five years old. My mother loved celebrating the birthday of America, her beloved country; it was her favorite holiday. She was the first person who told me the story of Crispus Attucks—a black man who was the first man to die in the Boston Massacre of 1770—and she let me know that many unnamed black people had fought and died beside white people in the American Revolution. She spoke to us of earning the right to be American, and how the Indian people, the Orientals, and the American Negro had helped build this country.

At the time, I listened to her without really understanding how important it was to her to be counted as an American. I didn't yet comprehend the seriousness of our condition as a people or the pain of being treated as throw-away people, as expendable. I did not know that black people could not legally go to the state parks and recreation centers on the Fourth of July because that was the day reserved for whites in Red River Parish. The sickness that gave birth to the idea of separating people along color lines had thus far escaped me, because I was so immersed in the loving womb of my family. Their love had protected me from the most blatant implications and limitations bred by the evils of an apartheid society.

Although the state parks were closed to blacks on the Fourth of July, they were open to blacks on June 19, or Juneteenth, which was considered Emancipation Day. In 1865, two years after President Abraham Lincoln signed the Emancipation Proclamation freeing black people, black people in Texas and many other parts of the South were finally told they were free. From what my mother always told me, black people all over Texas dropped whatever they were doing and left to celebrate their freedom. Maybe it was because she was a Texan and part Apache and Caucasian, but my mother never celebrated the 19th of June. She absolutely refused to celebrate Juneteenth, saying that many whites would like for us to think that our freedom was dependent on their declarations. She was very upset that blacks in Texas did not learn of their freedom until two years after the actual date of their emancipation. I remember her saying, "The day that I celebrate my freedom is the birth of America, because I am American—not the day that slaves were freed."

The Fourth of July proved to be my mother's favorite holiday. Even though she is no longer in her body, her strength, love, and energy live on. We have continued the family tradition of celebrating the Fourth of July, and we hold our family reunion almost every year on the Fourth.

During my childhood, while many black people celebrated the Fourth of July in their backyards, off our family would go to Black Lake, the local state park, to have a grand picnic with watermelons, fishing, barbecuing, potato salad, wonderful homemade cakes, and enough sodas to fill a tribe. One particular Fourth, an incident occurred that I remember as if it were yesterday. I witnessed a practical demonstration of the power and might of the feminine. My brothers and sisters were busy fishing or playing sports, but I was standing next to my mother while she cleaned some fish she had caught. In the distance, I could see a uniformed white man walking toward us, a park ranger for Black Lake. The ranger walked right up to my mother and asked her, "What are you doing here?"

My mother stood up and looked at him and said, "We are celebrating the Fourth of July." I was thinking that he had asked a stupid question, because I knew this was my mother's favorite holiday, and what else could we be doing but celebrating the Fourth? I stood there watching both of them.

The white man in uniform then told my mother, "You're not supposed to be here. The park is closed to coloreds today. You must leave."

My mother looked at him sternly and replied, "I am an American, and we are celebrating the Fourth of July today. If you want me to leave, you are going to have to bodily carry me and my twelve children out of here."

The ranger just stood looking at her, and she stared back at him, not blinking an eye. I watched in wonder as he stood there for a few moments, as if time had been suspended, then shook his head and turned to sneak away. I was amazed. He wasn't allowed to disturb our day, and my mother had demonstrated her absolute power. In my five-year-old mind, he had shrunk to about ten inches, and my mother had grown to be about ten feet tall.

That was a grand day, but I still didn't understand why the Fourth was so important to my mother. What I did understand was the power and might of the feminine principle. My mother was not a victim or a poor damsel in distress. She was an American, and I imagined that this was what it meant to be an American: to retain the right to choose your own heroes and to celebrate your own holidays, not special days that were set aside for you by others. Years would pass before I would really understand the depth of the strength and courage and sense of self that my mother manifested that day.

My father worked as a brick mason, and by 4:30 A.M. he would already have left for work. He was a gentle soul, and tended to defer most decision making to my mother. My father worked diligently with my brothers and trained them and many of the young men in our community to do his trade. He built our school, our community church, and many of the homes in and around our small town.

I once asked my older brother Bobby how my father had become a brick mason. Ever since I was born, my father had been a brick mason, and I thought he had always been a brick mason. Bobby shared with me the most wonderful story. Bobby is the second to the oldest of the twelve of us children, and the oldest son. He had worked with my father from early childhood. Originally, Dad had performed a series of jobs; he had worked as a sharecropper, a day laborer, and a logger. While working one winter as a logger, he became very ill with pneumonia and was bedridden for a time. Everyone was afraid that he was going to die. My mother cared for him as his fever raged. One morning, after many days of being very ill with an extremely high temperature, my father's fever broke, and he was able to wake up. He told our mother that he had had a dream that he was a brick mason and went on to describe the brick home he had built in his dream.

A few days later, he got up and began to draw the brick home he had built in his dream. Soon after he was completely well, he started working as a masonry attendant for a brick mason, a white man named Mr. Buffins. Daddy's task was to make the mortar, the material that is used to hold the bricks together. He was on his way to realizing his dream. Bobby told me that my father had a keen sense of observation and was very good at calculating the shapes and sizes of the bricks. With his strong work ethic, learning this new skill took no time at all. He was a quick worker and kept the mortar ready for Mr. Buffins to lay the bricks. Soon Dad was left on his own to make all the necessary preparations for laying the bricks properly. Mr. Buffins didn't realize that he was teaching my father all he needed to know about laying bricks. "Mr. Buffins was given to smoking and drinking," my brother told me, "and while he was away, Dad would pick up the trowel and lay a brick or two exactly next to the others." By practicing in this way, soon he was able to lay bricks like a professional. At home, he continued drawing brick homes and began designing chimneys. Within a few years, he was able to take on his own jobs. I was extremely impressed with our father's ability to bring his dream to fruition.

Our home in those days was located in the small, exclusively black section of town called Springville. Everyone knew one another or was related. I think we were the only family without any cousins in the school, but we didn't need any cousins because there were so many of us. Springville Elementary and High School was one school comprising kindergarten through twelfth grade. I still remember my first-grade teacher, a beautiful and impeccable black woman named Miss Ross. I wanted to be just like her. My ninth-grade English teacher was my eldest sister. From the time I entered the fifth grade on, she had been a teacher in our school. It was only recently that I started calling her by her first name and not Mrs. Gipson.

I had begun school in 1955, one year after the Supreme Court declared that separate was not equal and handed down the *Brown* v. *the Board of Education* decision. In 1955, Dr. Martin Luther King, Jr., led the Montgomery, Alabama, bus boycott, a refueling of the long struggle by Americans of African descent to fight for equal rights under the law. *Brown* v. *the Board of Education* supposedly ended the separate but equal rule. It informed all states in the Union that they could no longer maintain school systems that separated students along color lines.

The highest court in America had finally ruled against segregated schools, but at the time I began public school, the separation of black and white children wasn't even questioned. America's own apartheid system was viewed as the norm. The state of Louisiana was not conscious of the human rights issue, and the idea of desegregating the public schools was left untouched. No one talked about school integration, not even my mother, who had strong views and talked about almost every issue in life. She especially liked to talk about Dr. King; she loved the idea of what he was doing, but she feared for his life. Many times, so-called "ordinary black folk" would express the idea that young black people should just work hard, make a decent living, and leave white people to their ways.

In those years, apartheid was the rule in the state of Louisiana, and my perception of Louisiana today is that it was and still may be one of the most backward states in the United States. Its record on human rights and civil rights is among the poorest in the country. Today more than 60 percent of its black students still attend segregated schools. However, I must honestly say that I am not necessarily a proponent of forced integration, because I don't believe that people can be forced into accepting, supporting, and caring about one another across racial and other perceived barriers. Dissolving barriers and transforming relationships is heart work, and heart work cannot be legislated. It is possible to justify the thrust by both blacks and whites to stop forcing the issue of integration, since many black children have suffered as a result of forced desegregation.

When desegregation finally arrived in Louisiana in the early 1970s, it became another way of depriving black people of what they needed and deserved. Black students lost wonderful black teachers who loved them and were replaced by white teachers who resented being forced to teach in black schools. Most integrated schools were staffed by white teachers, who were not prepared emotionally to teach black students. Most white children were relocated to all-white private schools or placed in exceptional classes that were not available to blacks. I'm not sure which outcome was worse. The scars of this period are deep and painful, and I'm glad that I escaped them.

I went to an all-black school. The "N word" was not a word that young people used, because we viewed it as extremely derogatory. The school environment was filled with respect and love; it was a wonderful experience. Our teachers loved us and encouraged us to learn. While we lacked the up-to-date equipment and books of our white counterparts, this did not seem to hinder our teachers' ability to instill within us the thirst for knowledge. Our teachers gave us all they had. They taught us to love ourselves, and made sure we knew about early black leaders such as Harriet Tubman, Sojourner Truth, George Washington Carver, Booker T. Washington, Carter G. Woodson, and W. E. B. Dubois.

I very much valued the writings of Carter G. Woodson, especially his book *The Mis-Education of the Negro.* Woodson was a proponent of higher education, and at the same time warned us of the dangers and pitfalls of our system of education for the Negro. My mother shared Woodson's beliefs. She was determined that we go on to pursue an education, but she would warn us not to become "educated fools." She wanted us to be educated and to be able to earn a living, but she did not want us to forget the value of serving our community.

I knew that I would follow in my sisters' footsteps and go to Southern University or Grambling College. My eldest sister was beginning her higher education in 1955, the same year I started school. My schoolbooks were "hand-me-downs" from the white schools. They would get new books, and their used books would be passed on to us. Sometimes I would come home complaining about the condition of the books, because they would be all marked up or have pages ripped or hardbound covers torn off. I remember my mother commented, "Don't pay attention to the fact that white children don't know how to care for books; just make sure that you learn everything that is in them." She believed strongly in education, because she felt it opened doors to enter the mainstream of society. She believed in the American dream. She was afraid that if we weren't well educated, we would wind up working in a white woman's kitchen, and she informed us in detail of all the horrors of what happens to young black girls who had to work in white homes.

School was fun, and I worked hard to maintain the high standards set by my older sisters. It was an unspoken expectation that I would do well. It is amazing how children fulfill the expectations of the adults who are responsible for their development. I believed that there was nothing that I could not accomplish.

Nevertheless, the options and opportunities available to us were limited by our society. Because of the protection afforded me by my loving family and supportive teachers, I had not yet come into direct contact with the views of white Americans. I had not been socialized in a white environment, so my basic grounding was more oriented toward group support, respect for elders, and a sense of community rather than rugged, competitive individualism. Even though my parents were fiercely independent, they did not think only of themselves; they shared their skills with the community. My mother was responsible for opening the doors of opportunity for many young girls who would not be able to go to college but could learn to earn a living as a beautician.

I grew up feeling good about myself and my family. In 1966, the safe little enclave created by my parents and the community I lived in was still intact. Black people had their world, and white people had theirs. Life was relatively simple, and we didn't give much thought to the political arena. My mother, however, was concerned about the Voting Rights Act that had passed in 1965, and wondered if it would really go into effect. She had always been able to vote in the national election, but local elections were another matter. Local elections were the way whites maintained political power. She also knew that many black people had not been able to qualify to vote; there was always a long and ridiculous test to pass that had nothing to do with the candidates who were running or the election process.

The country was beginning to enact laws to address these wrongful and hurtful acts practiced against black people. However, most of us knew that "the more things change, the more they remain the same." Just as our schools continued to practice apartheid long after the Supreme Court ruled to eliminate segregation, many in our community felt that the new Voter Registration Act would have the same clout as all the other laws passed supposedly to uplift us: Namely, nothing would change.

The control of the local government by whites did not diminish our level of hope for our future in this country. We were Americans, and we were sure that one day we would realize the American dream. We knew instinctively that there was nowhere else we could go. We were Americans heart and soul.

My mother aimed all of her daughters toward the local black college and left her sons to my father to be trained as brick masons. Our daily lives were filled with work, school, and church. It was also clear to my mother that professional opportunities were limited in our small town, so we witnessed the exodus of my sisters one by one as they left for the North or the West to seek employment opportunities.

Early Messages

In the summer of 1966, the country was in the midst of the social turmoil and unrest that the 1960s are known for. Many African Americans were just beginning to make the transition from being referred to as Negro to demanding to be called African American or black. That summer found me on a bus on the way to California. I was leaving the sheltered, supportive cocoon of my family behind. Little did I know that I would never go home to live. As far as I knew, I was only to be away for the summer, because in the fall I would return to Springville High School to complete my senior year. After all, I would be class valedictorian. It was expected of me, and I had the grades to be named best in my class of 1967.

I was on my way to California to help one of my older sisters by keeping house for her family and looking after her three little boys while she and her husband worked evening jobs. The bus ride out was long and arduous, but I felt surprisingly safe for a lone young woman traveling for the first time on a three-day journey. I knew the rules—blacks were to drink out of certain fountains and use certain bathrooms since Louisiana had never bothered to change any of its apartheid rules. Signs everywhere still read "Whites only" or "Colored only." My mother cautioned me to pay attention to people's behaviors and I would be fine. She warned me as I got on the bus, "Common sense is not common to common people," and told me that I must remember how she had raised me. I got on the bus loaded with enough food and enough wisdom to see me through the ages.

As I sat at the back of the huge Greyhound bus, looking out the window as it slowly headed west to Texas, I was scarcely aware of the race separation issue and the whites seated in the front of the bus. Somehow I had almost completely ignored the whole issue of the separation of races. My mother had always explained to me that whites created separate schools because they were a lot like spoiled children and did not know how to share. So that was as far as the issue was addressed in our family.

As we passed through Texas, I was surprised when a middle-aged white man got on the bus and came to sit beside me. As I think about it now, I was not afraid. We had been taught to be friendly and respectful to everyone, because how you treat others would come back. Our parents believed in the law of compensation, and my father would say that life is like a boomerang: What you do will surely come back to you and usually when you least expect it.

I welcomed my new guest. I was just beginning to munch on some of the wonderful food I had carefully packed away. Out of courtesy, I offered the stranger some of my food. He looked at me oddly and said, "No, thank you," in his Texas accent. I thought immediately that he must be a cowboy because he had boots on. I wondered what he had done with his horse, since a cowboy is nothing without a horse. I followed my mother's advice exactly, paying close attention to the stranger's behaviors and comments. He appeared kind enough, even asking me, "Where are you goin'?" I answered briefly: "To California." He remarked, "You got a long trip," and that was the extent of our conversation. He was quiet for the rest of our trip. I was being careful to make sure I did nothing to offend this person. Now I realize that my mother's guidance had something to do with the fact that many times the livelihood and very lives of black people often depended on their having the keen sense to anticipate the attitude and behavior of whites long before white people were aware of their own attitudes, behaviors, needs, desires, and wants.

My trip was safe, and I enjoyed it immensely, especially Arizona, which I thought was an absolutely magical place. I remembered my mother's pride in her Indian heritage. As I mentioned earlier, my mother attributed her courage and temperament to her Apache blood. Many times she had told me that the American Negro owed a great deal to the Indians. She said that had it not been for the Indians helping Negroes to escape plantation life, marrying them and protecting them, many more of us would have died horrible deaths during the two and a half centuries of legalized slavery. Seeing the Indians not as my mother saw them, as braves standing strong and holding the ground that they walked on, but as a broken people, selling jewelry and blankets at the bus stop, caused me to feel some sadness, and I retreated to the bus, not wanting my idea of the American Indian to be shattered.

My bus finally arrived in downtown Palo Alto, California. We had driven across the Bay Bridge, which was the most beautiful thing I had ever seen. The City of San Francisco was a dream, the most famous city in the world. I could not imagine anything bad happening in a place like San Francisco. I had only gazed out my window to marvel at this jewel, and now I was greeted by my sister and brother-in-law and their three little boys. I settled into the family routine, preparing the breakfast for the boys and making sure the kitchen was clean and ready when my sister returned home from work.

As summer came to a close, my sister had grown to depend on my support. She had been offered a more lucrative job, but it was the 4:00 P.M. to midnight shift. They needed my help, so she made arrangements with my mother for me to stay on with them for my senior year. I would enroll in Ravenswood High School in the fall. My mother was a little reluctant since I would miss out on being class valedictorian and an automatic first-year scholarship to Southern University. But my sister needed me, and we persuaded my mother that it would be a good opportunity and that I could always come back to attend college locally after I graduated from high school.

In the fall of 1966, I began my senior year in a strange environment. The school was mixed, and almost all the teachers were white. My biggest concern was how to maintain my excellent grade point average. I was assigned a counselor who remarked, "Your grade point average is excellent. Why on earth would you come out here in your last year of school?" I didn't quite understand what she meant. I just asked her to please tell me what classes I needed in order to graduate. I was able to connect with a college-bound program, where we went to Stanford every Tuesday for tutoring and support from college students doing the community service of offering their skills to high school students who showed potential for a higher education. At the time, I was not thinking about going to a white institution, because it seemed that my soul already belonged to a "Negro" institution. I had promised my mother that I would be coming home at the end of the year to attend Southern University.

The school year moved quickly as I settled into my routine of going to school during the day and caring for my nephews in the evening. For a break, we would go to drive-in movies, which were absolutely marvelous. I thought back to the first time I went to the movies in Coushatta. There was a separate section for "colored" people. The "colored" section was always upstairs. I found it strange, because looking downstairs at the whites in the theater, they always looked so vulnerable. Someone could easily spit down or drop some other unmentionable substance on their heads. Of course, I would never do such a thing, even though I often thought of it.

The most difficult task I experienced the entire school year was the swimming test. During that time, the state of California had a swim test that all students had to pass in order to receive a high school diploma. One had to swim the length of the pool twice. I didn't realize that I could have gotten a doctor's excuse that would have freed me from this requirement. My two newest friends were identical twins. They were white and somewhat large, but I was only connecting with their essence. They lived near me, and many mornings they would wait to walk with me to school. Although I wasn't focused on their color, these were my first white friends. It is amazing to think back and witness how colorblind I was at the time. My friends were the type of people who played strictly by the rules, and they assured me that the swimming test would not be an obstacle for me.

I began my first swimming class with the pressure that I had to swim the length of the pool twice or I could lose four years of hard work. My swim coaches were not the kindest of people. They were unwilling to take into consideration my need for a little extra support given that I had grown up in a town with no swimming pools for blacks and, unlike my sisters, had not learned to swim in the fishing pond. When the time came for the swim test, I began my swim feeling some pressure but sure that I would pass. In the middle of my swim, however, I began to panic. I felt myself being pulled down by the water, and no matter how hard I worked, I was not going anywhere, just sinking deeper into the water. I began to raise my hand for my gym teacher to throw a long stick to me so I could pull myself out of the water. I looked at her and screamed for help, but she just stared back at me, her blue eyes cold and unmoving. I screamed again for the stick, and begrudgingly she threw it toward me. I pulled myself out of the pool and sat there stunned, wondering, "What was that all about? I could have drowned!" I felt a little bit fearful and uneasy about this behavior because I had nothing in my repertoire of experiences to help me understand it. I felt that it had something to do with power. I would later experience this behavior in many of my encounters with whites in positions of authority.

I was finally able to pass my swim test, but something inside me caused me to question this woman's behavior. My mother came to mind, warning me to pay attention to people's behaviors, telling me that people say many things but what really matters is "what one does." Mother often used to say, "Talk is cheap; it is what one does that counts."

Up until April 1967, my plan was to return home at the end of the school year. About a week before my birthday, however, I received a letter from a representative of the University of California at Berkeley, stating that they had been at Ravenswood High in hopes of recruiting students for their Equal Opportunity Program. They had noticed my excellent records. They went on to say that I had taken most of the required college-bound courses, except the foreign language requirement, but that would not pose a problem if I was interested in applying. I immediately went to my sister with the exciting news. She was worried about the financial responsibility, but I was very interested. I could live on my own and educate myself with the help of the Equal Opportunity Program. I knew that my mother would love it. At the time I was not aware that then Governor Edmund G. Brown was trying to right a wrong committed by land grant higher institutions all over the state, which had practiced discrimination by not admitting eligible blacks, Hispanics, and Asians.

My mother had some concerns about my remaining in California. Unbeknownst to me, our father had had some health problems, and my mother finally gave in to my requests because it would ease some of the financial pressure if I received financial support to continue my education at the University of California. In the fall of 1967, I started my first year of college. This was an exciting period in America. All over the United States, students were making their voices heard. The free speech movement was in full bloom on campus. Straight out of the backwoods of Louisiana, I found this an unusual and extremely exciting experience. All I could think of was that I would start my preparatory studies for my future. I had always wanted to be a social worker; I believe my mother had inspired me in this direction because of her natural counseling skills.

In addition to receiving inspiration from my mother to become a social worker, I had always been interested in the human ability to create and maintain positive social bonds through community experiences. Therefore, it was very natural for me to choose to study the social sciences as a student. As I started school in the fall at the University of California at Berkeley, I left my childhood behind me and began my first steps into adulthood.

Kokomon's Early Years

In the Hammattan season of 1949, a little boy was born to Nii Korley and Ayorkor of the Ga Tribe in a fishing village called Gamashie in Ghana, West Africa. It was in the month of December, when the dry hot air blows across the Sahara Desert toward the Atlantic Ocean. It was a Saturday morning, and the mood in this African fishing village was festive, for this was the last day of the old year and the coming of the new year.

By oldest tradition, seven days from the day one is born, the outdooring-naming ritual takes place. At dawn, after the crowing of the cocks, my parents, Nii Korley and Ayorkor, took me out into the family compound under the African stars and the moon, and gathered with all my extended family to complete the naming ritual. A medicine man named Atta Ajabah held me up and pointed me to the African sky and prayed. He then placed me on the red earth and prayed. I was made to taste first water, then akpeteshie, a local concoction of aged sugarcane. Finally, the medicine man poured libation to invoke the spirit of all my ancestors and said, "Eyes but no eyes, ears but no ears, may this child respect and honor our ancestors and all beings, and may the village people bless this child with these gifts: love and affection, trust, compassion, and kinship. This child came to this earth with black chunky hair, and when the African sun turns purple on his last days, may he leave from this earth with white chunky hair." At the end of the prayer, the entire extended family responded, "Dzoa," which means "Let it be so." Three words were whispered in my ears: "Korkwei," because I was third born by ranking order; "Kwame," because I was born on a Saturday; and lastly "Blonya," because I was born on New Year's Eve. My full legal name then was Halifax Korkwei Clottey, and I was also known by the nicknames from my naming ceremony, Kwame and Blonya. Years later, I became known by my musical stage name, Kokomon.

One by one the family members gave the medicine man money with a message for Korkwei, which symbolized their commitment to the well-being of the newborn baby.

A long time ago, but not too long, my father told me the story of a man of great wealth and social importance. He was called Anunsah Klotay, and he was my grandfather. He was responsible for enthroning chiefs. He was engaged in many enterprises, including importing and fishing. He married four wives, who bore him twenty children. My people believed that the wealth of a village was its people. Because of this belief, Anunsah Klotay justified a tribe of his own.

I was born into a family of fourteen, including six half-brothers and sisters. My father was a businessman who manufactured soda pop and also engaged in import and export, as had his father who went before him. Due to his economic and social standing, my father also assumed responsibility for his three sisters. It was not enough for him to take care of his immediate family, for by tradition he was involved in the network of tribal obligations and responsibilities toward an extended family. My aunts were also industrious and had enterprises of their own.

My mother, besides being our caretaker, was herself a trader who manufactured a special food called kenkey. At five feet tall, my mother issued precise orders like a sea captain. This paraphrase of a Bible quote best describes her: "She opened her mouth with wisdom, and her tongue was like the law of kindness. She looked well to the ways of her household, and did not eat of the bread of idleness." In short, my mother was a visionary whose middle name could have been "audacious."

My parents were good Christians, and claimed membership in the bosom of the infallible Methodist church. Bible studies were extremely important in my home. At the same time, both my parents were deeply rooted in the African spiritual codes and ancestral worship, which complemented their involvement in the Methodist church. My people saw the Bible as an observation of what they already knew. For them, becoming a part of the church was simply a way to join with our European brothers and sisters in their way of communicating with God. African rituals and ancestral worship, however, were what connected my people with God. For example, it is the belief of the Ghanaian people that it is always a blessing to express love and hospitality to all visitors. They believe that when a person dies, this does not end their membership in the society. Respect for those who have passed on is a deep spiritual practice known as ancestral worship. Ancestral worship is based on the belief that when members of the family die they go to heaven, or a state of peace, and from there they send blessings to the survivors and finally reincarnate. Ghanaians also believe that whenever visitors come, they travel with three unseen ancestors. And so, in order not to offend any of these ancestors, their presence is always acknowledged, as they can bring either blessings or curses depending upon the way they are treated.

Eight rains passed, and at eight years of age in addition to attending school, I was drawn to other things children did in the village. For example, on weekends we would go mango hunting, which was really mango stealing. We would go from farm to farm, just little boys being mischievous. One day when we were hunting mangos, we came upon a huge owl, right at noontime. I knew it was noontime, because even though we didn't have wristwatches in Ghana, all we had to do was watch our shadows to know the time, and at noontime there is no shadow, for the center of the sun is right on the zenith of your head. Anyhow, we saw a beautiful owl, and as we shouted at it, "Witch, witch, witch, witch bird," it swooped down very quickly and as it came back up into the air it had a big snake, which it released over our heads, and we all went running. I'm not sure what happened to me, but by the time I got home I was bleeding, perhaps from stepping on some broken glass. So that was the end of my mango hunting.

On summer vacations, my brothers and I, together with my cousins, engaged ourselves at my father's soda pop factory. We were compensated with soda pop. We would sell some of it for cash and keep the remainder. This was also true during the Christmas holidays. In so many ways, I learned in my family's bosom the value of hard work and partnership.

From an early age, I displayed a great interest in other religions. My spiritual quest had begun. When I was eight or nine, a Catholic invited me to see what the Catholic church was all about. On a sunny day, I attended church with him. I couldn't believe that I spent half of the time on my knees, and when I got home my knees were sore. I couldn't understand the Latin parts of the mass, so that was it for me for Catholicism. About a year later, my elder brother, Nii Klotey, who at the time was an orthodox Muslim, strongly suggested that I and a couple other brothers be initiated. When I learned that once I was initiated I would have to pray to God in Arabic, I was very dismayed by the idea that I would have to converse with God in a language I didn't understand, so I decided that Islam was not the path for me. "If God does not understand my African language, he should find me the God who would," I said to myself. Nevertheless, I was initiated in Islam, and my name was Yusef, which translates as Joseph.

Overall, growing up in Africa was a wonderful experience. Under the British, Ghana had been known as the Gold Coast, because they had discovered much gold there. While the Gold Coast was a colony, the national anthem was "God Save the Queen," but after independence we got a new national anthem, an authentic African composition. This was important to me, because our prime minister, Kwame Nkrumah, advocated a sense of kinship with all Africans and all black people in the world, at least in theory. This was a time of pride in being African, that it is all right to be who you are.

Although I was not particularly conscious of the political situation as a child, I do remember that in 1957, when I was nine years old, Kwame Nkrumah led the country to independence from British colonial rule. This momentous occasion drew world dignitaries, such as Martin Luther King, Jr. Kwame Nkrumah created a system of free education in Ghana, and I enjoyed going to school. Growing up in a British colony, I had to learn English, because the school system was conducted in English, not Ga.

At ten years of age, I had an important dream. In this dream, I received a huge sum of money to use to create joy for children as a healing tool. Although the enormity of the sum of money shocked me, I knew that one is never given a dream without the ability to fulfill it. However, a succession of questions flooded my mind: Why a child like me? How would this come to pass? And so on. As these questions haunted me, I sought refuge in my mother's wisdom. "Don't worry," she counseled me. "God will show you how it will happen."

My dream as a child included the idea that somehow, someday, I would travel to the United States. And the African gods confirmed that when I was ready, when the time was right for me, I would find my way to America.

Throughout my childhood, I remained fascinated with America. At sixteen, I dreamed of being taken to America in a giant iron bird, and I had a sense that it would be in America that my mission would begin. For this reason, I always paid special attention to news of the United States. When my mother saw how adamant I was about my dream to one day go to the States, she agreed that someday I would go there, and she started calling me PaPa Abrochi, which means Mr. America.

After I finished elementary school, I went to secondary school, a technical college. I had always loved music, and I had always planned to be a musician someday. As a young man, some friends and I put a band together and modeled it after the Beatles. We were called the Termites, which still amuses me. Of course, this decision was heavily influenced by European models. I sometimes consider those years of loss, because I wanted to play music like the Beatles and look like them, but of course I couldn't ever look like Paul McCartney or Ringo Starr. There was a way in which the British imposed their culture over us Africans, as they did in all their colonies. In response, the Ghanaian people somehow felt that their own culture wasn't good enough.

Eventually, I was employed at the Star Hotel as a resident musician. While playing with the band at the hotel, I still held onto my dream of one day going to America. I had no idea how it would happen, but fate had it that music would be the vehicle that would bring me to the United States. I was told that this remarkable development was written in the handbook of providence. I continued working at the Star Hotel with a band for close to seven years, and this gave me the opportunity to meet many wonderful people. A couple of the people I met, upon learning I was interested in going to America, helped set me up with an educational scholarship. Another offer was to bring my entire band to the States. I thought it would be so much fun to travel with my band instead of going all by myself. Soon thereafter, in 1977, I went to the United States with my band. And that was the beginning of a new life for me.

Exercise for Exploring Your History

In this chapter, we have shared with you some of the experiences that shaped our early lives. In our journey toward racial healing, we have found that as we explore our personal histories, we create a space within our hearts and minds that allows us to let go of our painful past and reclaim our lost innocence. We invite you to join with us in this process of remembering and reclaiming your history, which will give you the groundwork for making the changes you desire in order to heal your attitudes toward race.

You can do this work alone, or if you have a group of friends or family you trust, you can invite them to join you in exploring and reconstructing your personal history. You may choose to do the exercises in this book by yourself, or you may choose to create a Healing Racism Circle, as described in Chapter 16.

1. Write an outline that describes your early years, or reflect on a brief biography of your early life. What were the formative experiences? You might want to chart them on a large piece of paper.

2. All of us were innocent of racial prejudice when we were children. What happened? Ask yourself the following important questions:

- When did you first become aware of race?

- What were the messages about your own race you received growing up—from your family, from your friends, from society?

- What messages did you receive growing up about other races—from your family, from your friends, from society?

- When did you first become aware of racial prejudice?

- What was the racial and ethnic composition of the community where your grew up? Did you encounter diversity in your neighborhood, your church or temple, or your school?

- What attitudes did you learn in your childhood that now call out for healing?

3. We have found in our workshops on healing racism that art can be very transformative. You might want to get out a drawing pad and some colored crayons or pens, and record with images the personal orientation you received growing up about race. You can draw images and symbols that stand for the messages you received. Sometimes pictures allow images to emerge that you cannot put into words.

4. After drawing these images, you can continue the healing process by re-creating and reframing each image. Allow yourself to draw the corresponding healing image for each of the pictures you have already made. If you

are in a group, this is the time to share the images with a friend. If you are doing this on your own, you can jot down thoughts and insights as you freely associate on your symbols. Many people have used this process to reclaim their lost innocence. We believe that we can all learn to be as little children once again, and free ourselves of the judgments, blame, and guilt of our past.

CHAPTER TWO

Separation and Selfhood

*The world can teach no images unless you want
to learn them. There will come a time when
images have all gone by, and you will see
you know not what you are. It is to this unsealed
and open mind that truth returns, unhindered
and unbound. Where concepts of the self have been
laid by is truth revealed exactly as it is. When every
concept has been raised to doubt and question,
and been recognized as made on no assumptions
that would stand the light, then is the truth left
free to enter in its sanctuary, clean and free of guilt.
There is no statement that the world
is more afraid to hear than this:
I do not know the thing I am, and therefore do not
know what I am doing, where I am, or how to
look upon the world or on myself.
Yet in this learning is salvation born.
And What you are will tell you of Itself.*

A COURSE IN MIRACLES

In this chapter, we continue to share with you the stories of
our lives as we entered young adulthood and came into our
selfhood. Along the way, we also experienced the pain of separation. Again, as you read our stories, consider your own
journey into young adulthood and the ideas that you adopted
as your own about race.

Aeeshah's Journey Continues

The University of California at Berkeley turned out to be a great learning ground for racial disharmony. My first roommate in the dorms was a young Chinese woman who never spoke to me. Coming from the South, I found this extremely difficult because a basic courtesy given to everyone where I grew up, black or white, was "Good morning, ma'am," or "Good evening, sir." I didn't understand my new roommate's silence. After only a week with me, she mysteriously moved. I came back to the room after a morning class to find her room clean as a whistle with all her things gone. Later I learned that she had moved to the fifth floor. About two weeks later, I got another new roommate, who was Japanese. She also treated me with disdain and moved out very quickly. Growing up in the South, I had never encountered Asians before, and I didn't know how to interpret these brief encounters.

These roommate changes occurred in the first month of the first quarter. For the rest of the quarter, I enjoyed the privilege of having a room all to myself. This solace ended at the beginning of the second quarter. My new roommate was white and seemed overly friendly. I became a little suspicious of her, and I found myself using the tactics of my first two roommates: remaining silent in reaction to her overtures. She soon moved because I did not respond to any of her gestures of friendship. During those days, the university did not have any conscious plan for creating a dialogue or encouraging exchanges among the new and diverse groups assembled on campus. I'm not sure if the university was even a willing participant in the assembly of its colorful new recruits. It was like a great accidental experiment.

Even more than my dorm experience, it was my classes that had the deepest impact and set the tone for my entire stay at U.C. Berkeley. I quickly began to learn that this was not a user-friendly environment for people of color. My first sociology class was taught by a professor who became a nameless, faceless, oppressive Caucasian from my perspective. The class had about a hundred students, which was small for the university at that time. Many of our classes contained a thousand students or more, over 90 percent of them white. It is amazing to think back on this now, because I was not so color-conscious at the time.

The professor was my teacher of the value of ethnicity. His first question to the class provided a rude awakening. He stood very erect, with an air of superiority, holding his pointed nose high above everyone else, and asked, "How many WASPs are there in the class?" I was a little taken aback by the question, which seemed so out of context. I wondered how any of those little stinging insects could have found their way into the lecture hall. I definitely knew about these kinds of wasps, because I had been stung many times trying to get peaches from the trees in the woods behind my home in Louisiana.

I looked around the class and noticed that people were raising their hands. I was very confused, and I asked myself if I was the only person unsure of what he meant. I wondered if the others were also raising their hands for clarification, and I decided to join in the questioning. In addition to my confusion, I was also thinking of my mother, who had always warned me never to be afraid to ask a question, even if you felt that you might be perceived as stupid. She had always said that the only stupid questions are the ones that are left unasked.

41

As I raised my hand, the professor looked at me curiously and disdainfully and asked, "What do you want?" I felt a little fear for the first time, but I moved past it to ask my question. I was unsure of my feelings and felt that I was somehow intruding. At that moment, I felt that maybe I was the only person in class who was confused. I stood up and rather hurriedly asked my question: "What do you mean by wasp?"

The professor looked very coldly through me and answered, "White Anglo-Saxon Protestant, of course." I received the tone of his voice like a blow in the pit of my stomach. I slumped down in my chair. Looking around the room, I observed that many of the students were laughing. I noticed for the first time that I was the only black person in this class, and that many of the hands raised were clearly WASPs. I felt that I had done something terrible by asking the question, and I felt deeply embarrassed that I hadn't known what a WASP was. Apparently, a WASP was a very important thing to be in this professor's class. This was my initiation into the university system at Berkeley.

A similar tone pervaded most of my required classes for the social science field major. I was being taught that black people were second-class citizens, somehow inferior and a social burden for our country. They were the fringe, castaways of society, throw-away people who must be helped because they did not know how to help themselves. The social worker would be their guide. This patronizing and condescending attitude that social workers must acquire in order to help their clientele was very difficult for me. Sitting in class and hearing the myriad of negative descriptions of people of color was a very painful process for me. I could feel anger seeping into my personality. The separation and isolation that this environment bred with regard to the non-white population were extremely harmful.

I began a psychological process of rejecting this kind of negative imagery and instruction about black people. I became involved in the struggle to bring a more accurate portrayal of the achievements of black people to the institution. This involved fighting actively for an ethnic studies department on campus to include African American, Native American, and Asian American studies. This department was to provide a safety net for students of color, a place where their self-esteem could be rebuilt and nurtured after the wider academic and social structure tore them down.

I became involved in the Black Students Union, picketing the university for the development of an ethnic studies department, working part-time to pay for my essentials while attending school, and connecting with other students who wanted change in the university. We also participated in other demonstrations to build support for our cause on campus.

It was interesting how easy it was to continue the segregation process on a mostly all-white campus. The few white students I had reached out to at the beginning of my studies at the university soon grew to be distant memories. Connecting with students who were racially different became an impossible task, and I withdrew totally from trying to socialize across the color line. As I look back on it, I realize that this institution was designed to increase isolation, separation, and fear among the various groups on campus. This was not the academic setting I had envisioned for myself. Instead of growing wiser, I was growing more fearful.

The balance of my academic years was spent rejecting the social environment, the attitudes of the professors, the basic goals of the administration and trustees, and more important, the curriculum. I found the fabric of this particular Eurocentric institution quite toxic to my growth.

The challenge that was most difficult for me was not the academic demands, but the obviously negative beliefs about black Americans, which were being taught in the historical, social, and political context of my classes. The attitudes of the professors and the unspoken implication of the inferiority of blacks backed by an array of statistics were clearly amplified in lectures and seminars. According to the sociologists and political scientists of the day, black people were on the fringes of society because of some inherent inferiority or lack of the intellectual, cultural, and organizational skills necessary to be self-determining or to build positive communities. A constant stream of ideas depicting the wretchedness of black life was being taught as a means of preparing young people entering service professions with the intent of helping these "poor" people.

I knew from personal experience that I was not dependent. My father and mother had run their own businesses in one of the poorest states in the Union. They provided for twelve children, and as the youngest I had never thought of myself as poor, deprived, or incapable. My parents had worked very hard to provide for us physically as well as emotionally. We had no awareness of welfare. What was welfare? In Coushatta, Louisiana, the government stipends were not meant for blacks; they were only given to indigent whites.

By the time of my graduation from the university, I was one angry black woman. I wanted nothing to do with this society! The American dream of a just society was truly just a dream. Or, as James Baldwin stated more eloquently in his book *The Fire Next Time:* "The American dream has therefore become something much more closely resembling a nightmare, on the private, domestic, and international levels." The

44

American dream had never been realized and would never be realized by people of color. We could work to be as white as we wanted to be. The door to acceptance and justice would always be closed. I thought back to my mother and her love for America and wondered why she so loved this country which had no love for her.

African Americans were truly an American-made product. We came out of the bowels of this country. We took the worst that America offered to us and transformed it into wealth for the entire nation. The only original musical scale that this country can boast of came out of the pain and sorrow of African Americans. In numerous fields of endeavor, African Americans helped to make the United States a uniquely creative country.

Underneath my anger was pain—the pain of every African American who experiences the abuse, rejection, and fear that our country inflicts upon us. Most Europeans who came to America escaped the oppression of their countries, but African Americans stayed and tried to assimilate and attain the American dream that was held out to them but was always out of reach. Even if African Americans became wealthy financially, they were somehow never accepted fully as human.

Looking back on this period in my life, I am reminded how devastating racism can be. Several years ago, I read an interview with Wimbledon tennis champion Arthur Ashe in *People* magazine. When asked by the interviewer whether his AIDS diagnosis was the heaviest burden he had ever had to bear, Ashe replied, "AIDS isn't the heaviest burden I have had to bear." The interviewer dug deeper, asking, "Is there something worse? Your heart attack?" Ashe finally responded, "Being black is the greatest burden I've had to bear. No question about it. Race has always been my biggest burden. Having to

45

live as a minority in America. Even now it continues to feel like an extra weight tied around me."

So it was back when I was attending the university. The concepts that black people were deprived, unfit for self-determination, inherently inferior, and unable to bring themselves into the mainstream of American life began to wear on my emotional fabric. I was appalled, and my anger grew. I did not believe in any of these concepts. The academic content being taught to me as a black American was lethal as far as I was concerned. To be educated in a Eurocentric environment meant that I had to distance myself emotionally from my own community. I had to imitate the larger white society by expressing and professing its views. Most damaging was the concept that being born black was not a positive phenomenon of nature. This is the root of the miseducation of a whole race of people in our society. This was also the wedge that facilitated the beginning of my personal choice to live a life whose boundaries were based on race.

I was not able to reconcile my feelings of anger with how I would serve in the society where I was born. I felt betrayed. I was not willing to stay in the university system any longer, because I saw it as the place where the demise, murder, and dehumanization of indigenous peoples were supported and explained in clinical and academic terms. I was not comfortable in this setting, and I had made a commitment to myself never to loan my mind and heart to another Eurocentric-focused higher institution of learning. The thought of moving further in this setting would mean selling out all that I had left, which was my self-respect.

I faced a dilemma as I contemplated what would come next. I was dispirited as I considered my prospects. One day on campus, a friend excitedly shared with me that an unusual speaker would be appearing at the International House. His name was Louis Farrakhan, the spokesperson for the Nation of Islam. I had become intrigued with the Nation of Islam when I did a comparative study on Martin Luther King, Jr., and Malcolm X for one of my sociology classes. I knew about the Nation of Islam's work and was impressed with what they were doing in Chicago and other urban centers in terms of social reform, moral uplift, and economic empowerment. Nevertheless, I had never ventured to any of the mosques located near the university. There was one in East Oakland, and another in San Francisco.

So I went to hear Minister Louis Farrakhan at the International House and was extremely impressed with his presentation. All of my confusion about my experience at the university was explained in his ninety-minute lecture. Minister Louis Farrakhan is an eloquent speaker. He logically outlined why white Americans would never accept black Americans as equals no matter how much education or money we acquired. He went on to say that white people just didn't have it in them, that they were diabolical and evil. He said that they were devils and that nothing we did could change their behavior. He went on to point out historically all the things that African Americans have done to support the American system, and how each time our reward has been a slap in the face.

I sat there thinking, "This man is right." This is what I had been trying to do: to be accepted by someone who could never accept me, and worse yet, could not even acknowledge my humanity. I felt relieved. I knew what I had to do. I had received my answer. I would no longer strive to be accepted by a group of people who could not accept me. I had skills, and I wanted to serve, so I began the process of deliberately separating myself from white society.

That weekend, I went to my first mosque meeting at 82nd and MacArthur Boulevard. It was very different from anything I had ever encountered. I walked in the door and observed all the women in white floor-length garments with head scarves on. They were immaculately clean. They ushered me in. I was a little uncomfortable, because everyone who came in had to be searched. The men and the women were separated. I wondered whether this was what I wanted, but once I got in, the speaker started speaking. I had become more intensely aware of my blackness, and I began to feel that the only option for me was to become a member of the Nation of Islam, a religious, separatist organization that professed black self-help concepts and self-responsibility. I found the idea of uplifting poor blacks in the slums and ghettoes of America inspiring, even awesome, in its implications. That day, hearing Minister Farrakhan's message refreshed me, and I allowed his words to quench my thirst. I felt he was speaking truth—truth I had not heard during my four years at the university.

The other side of the Nation of Islam's philosophy was based upon a religious and mythical belief that European Caucasian whites were devils, evil to the core, who would never treat people of color fairly. White people's sole aim was to dominate and enslave people of color through institutional and economic racism. This offered a solution to my problem of where to invest my energies as a young American. I looked back into history and cited all the horrors that had been wrought on us as a people. I did not have to look back very far to find examples of maltreatment, for there were many present-day and historical indicators of brutality and abuse.

I made a serious decision at this point in my young life. I began to fear and hate others because of their racial origin and the misdeeds of their ancestors. I became an active member of the Nation of Islam. I taught school in this organization for almost seven years. I consciously separated myself from white America. I became a living example that the races could not live harmoniously, loving and supporting one another's growth. Separation of the races became a norm for me by personal choice.

During these years, there was much that was positive that I experienced and shared. The Nation of Islam spoke eloquently of what we could achieve if we could only unite as a people, if we could only learn to love ourselves. The teaching pointed out the ways American blacks had been taught self-hatred, and out of this self-hatred we were forcing ourselves to integrate, out of the mistaken desire to become more white, as if that would somehow make us better. Instead, the Nation of Islam was encouraging all black people to wake up to the knowledge of what they were as human beings and stop being puppets of the American system.

As the Nation of Islam spoke out against integration, I weighed and balanced its ideas against my experience at the university. My young mind felt that these people were right, that I would never be able to learn to do for myself by listening to the guidelines set for me by this society. The more I listened, the less I wanted to continue to be part of this system. I began to resent all white institutions and what they represented. I wanted to be at the temple. I wanted to be one of the black Muslims who were always shining and feeling good about themselves, who felt that we as a people were worth it. They spoke eloquently of moving into the community, while most educated blacks were moving out of the community. I was very touched by this whole experience, and I knew I could never be the same. After several months of attending services at the mosque, I decided I wanted to become a member of the Nation of Islam and to give up my so-called Negro name. Elijah Muhammad, the leader of the Nation of Islam, taught that we did not know our own name, that we were given these names by white people, and that our original names were taken away from us.

I looked back into the life of Thomas Jefferson, and I felt sick when I learned of his exploits. I was embarrassed to be an American. The more I delved into what this country has done to people of color, the more I lost the pride that my mother had. I lost my innocence. I wanted nothing more to do with this society. And that meant giving up the name that was given to me by my mother. So I wrote my mother and told her that I was going to become a Muslim and change my name. I was going to give up my slave name. She wrote back saying, "What do you mean, slave name?"

And I wrote back telling her that when we black people came to America we had names that were not these westernized European names, but African names. I told her we could reclaim our African names, but first we had to give up the white man's name. My mother found this all very confusing, and she gave me a piece of her mind. My mother was very concerned about me and afraid I was heading for trouble.

I remember my mother telephoning me early one morning for the explicit purpose of giving me one of her famous talks on the strength we must have to be successful right alongside white folks, and how prayer could help. As I listened to my mother, I was thinking to myself that she was really just a lost Negro, mentally dead, who didn't know any better. So I listened to everything she said while shaking my head on the other end of the phone. When the conversation ended, I sat down and wrote my letter of acceptance—a letter that every black person who wanted to become part of the Nation of Islam had to write. It was a very serious letter to write because it meant that I was making a commitment to the ideas and the creed of the Nation of Islam, that I was making a commitment to the black nation here in the "belly of the beast," as they called America. Living in America was considered hell for black Americans, and we had to strive to live in this country but not be of this country, to try as much as possible to be a nation within a nation.

My letter went like this: "Dear Savior Allah, deliver us. I have attended the teachings of Islam two or three times as taught by one of your ministers. I believe in it. I bear witness that there is no God but thee, and that Mohammed is thy servant and apostle. I desire to reclaim my own name. Please give me my original name. My slave name is as follows." I ended my letter and accepted my X. I did not yet have my Islamic name, so I was known as Patsy X.

My life became one of a dedicated Muslim. I would arise every morning at 5:00 A.M. and do my ablutions and prayer. I adhered to all the rules and laws of the Nation of Islam, including dietary restrictions. We focused on our mission—ways that we could buy farmland, grow our own food, open up our own schools, and teach and educate our own. As Elijah Muhammad used to say, "Why be like a dog waiting for crumbs under the table of the white man when you can go out and hunt and fend for yourself?" I loved all this talk of self-sufficiency. I loved devoting my life to the community one hundred percent during the seven years I worked and lived as a black Muslim.

I had mostly separated myself from my family, who did not quite understand my beliefs, and from my previous friends, except for those who joined the Nation of Islam with me.

They, too, had been alienated by being thrust into this hostile environment, and they were looking for something similar to their protective home environment. The Nation of Islam became our life.

I would teach school for seven hours every day, and then I would go to the bakery and work there for a few hours, or to the sewing factory and work there. I was proud to be working to build a Nation of our own.

Our ultimate goal was complete separation from the white man. The Nation of Islam felt that white people never could and never would treat black people equally. I think back to watching Louis Lomack's documentary about the Nation of Islam called *The Hate That Hate Produced.* But despite the racial separation advocated and the derogatory analysis of white people, the day-to-day life of people in the community of black Muslims was about love, not hate. It was about a group of people learning to love themselves. As I look back on this period of my life, I recognize that it was a very powerful awakening experience for me that helped propel me into a life of service.

At the time, I thought I would be part of this community for the rest of my life. Little did I know that my journey into the Nation of Islam was not an end but a beginning of my spiritual opening and my path to healing.

Kokomon in America

I had fulfilled my childhood dream and found myself in America. My band and I had arrived in New York in 1977, and we were staying in the Bronx. I found New York to be densely populated, dirty, and noisy. We were hosted by a Jamaican woman who was married to a Chinese man. It was quite a shock for me to be in this country, and this was when I first became aware of the issue of racism.

It is worth noting that prior to my coming to the United States, I had no racial stereotypes about white people or black people. I shared this opinion of Dr. Howard Thurman: "It is my belief that in the presence of God there is neither male nor female, white nor black, Gentile nor Jew, Protestant nor Catholic, Hindu, Buddhist, nor Moslem, but a human spirit stripped to the literal substance of itself before God."

We were living in the Bronx on a street called Sedgwick Avenue. My first sight of how black people lived in Harlem left me speechless. Many people were begging, and conditions were not as I had envisioned. I had thought that life in America was sweet for everyone. By that I mean that I believed that an evil such as homelessness would never exist here. I had grown up imitating James Brown, and playing all his songs. My other heroes included Wilson Picket, Tina Turner, Aretha Franklin, and Lena Horne. Ray Charles was also one of my favorites. All my life I had wanted to grow up to become a black American. Even in Ghana, I played all the contemporary music of black Americans. I thought that life in America was the best for black Americans. It wasn't until I was actually in New York that I witnessed the separation, the racial divide, and the poverty that afflicted American society.

When I completed my initial contract in New York, I had another contract with Hedzoleh Sound, the band that Hugh Masekela brought from Ghana sometime back. This was in Oakland, California. While I was playing with this band, one night I met a woman I will call Miss White, to avoid any embarrassment. She and I fell in love, and everything was wonderful, but no one had warned me about white people and the race problem in America.

One might ask how it was possible for me to fall in love with a white American. Ralph Waldo Emerson once wrote: "See, in any house where virtue and self-respect abide, the palpitation which the approach of a stranger causes." All of me surrendered to this process. When love beckoned I could not turn my back. As Kahlil Gibran wrote, "If in your fear you would seek only love's peace and love's pleasure, then it is better for you that you cover your nakedness and pass out of love's threshing-floor, into the seasonless world where you shall laugh, but not all your laughter, and weep, but not all your tears." At the moment when love struck me, I saw no color.

I might also add that three months into our dating, Miss White let me know that she was pregnant with my child. To bring honor and respect upon her, we both thought it was time to get married. So I proposed to her, and she agreed to marry me. She told her friends and family that this was what she wanted to do.

We set a date for the wedding, but when the day came, nobody from her side attended. Her parents didn't come, her brothers and sisters didn't come, and her friends didn't come. Only my African friends came to the ceremony. It was to be a day of celebration and joy and love, and no one from her side showed up. I believe it was very hard on both of us. In my culture, not coming to a wedding was a taboo, since the message was that the marriage was not approved.

Our marriage ended up being very short, lasting only approximately ninety days, due to the racial pressure that we experienced. One cold and silent morning, I came home from work and entered my apartment. Usually when I arrived, a warm air caressed my black African face, but not that day. The room was cold and totally empty. The echo of a sad voice seemed to hang in the air. Shocked that everything we possessed was gone, at first I assumed we had been robbed. But where was my pregnant wife? I searched every room, but she was gone.

Suddenly, an ancient emotion of anger and sadness began to stir inside me like a killer tropical storm. I was distraught beyond belief. I plunged myself onto my naked, cold bed, completely lost in a dream. I wondered whether I should call the police. But immediately I asked myself: Whose side would the police be on? Was I prepared to answer insane questions from men in uniforms? I was consumed by anger and hate. "He who hates has to show his hate in appropriate action and behavior; in a sense, he has to become hate," Franz Fanon had said. Was this what I wanted? I was left with no clear reasons for this madness. Suddenly, sleep came and took me away to such depth that I was lost in a much deeper dream.

When I awoke I realized that my wife had packed up everything in the house and taken flight. She was gone, and I would never see her again. This left me in a state of mistrust toward Americans, particularly white Americans. In 1996, I finally heard from somebody who told me that my ex-wife had passed away, so I prayed for her.

The breakup of my marriage and my direct experience of racism finally drove me just about insane. I used alcohol to deaden the pain. I ended up homeless, and a Chinese American man offered me an apartment. He was a very spiritual man, and he adopted me into his family. He began to assist me in very kind ways, educating me about the American culture. The way he reached out to me felt very African; in Ghana, that's the way it is.

One day I ran across a classified advertisement about studying theosophy. I was rather suspicious about God at that time in my life, but I was down and out, so I ordered the meditation course by mail and started my daily lessons. A version of the Prayer of Saint Francis of Assisi came with my meditation home study:

Lord, make me an instrument of thy peace.
Where there is hate, may I bring love.
Where offense, may I bring pardon.
May I bring union in place of discord.
Truth, replacing error.
Faith where once there was doubt.
Hope, for despair.
Light, where there was darkness.
Joy to replace sadness.
Make me not to so crave to be loved as to love.
Help me to learn that in giving I may receive.
In forgetting self, I may find life eternal.

SAINT FRANCIS OF ASSISI

As I started my healing process, my band went to Los Angeles to perform. I liked Los Angeles. The climate reminded me of Ghana, with its warm, balmy air, palm trees, and beaches. In 1978, I decided to relocate to Los Angeles. I was then about a year old in America, and I had already tasted the American "nightmare," lost a wife and a baby, and experienced the rejection and pain that racism breeds. I continued my meditations and gradually began to heal.

In Los Angeles, I discovered a music conservatory that interested me. In my composition program, I was the only black and the only African. This school gave me my first experience with a group of Americans who were primarily white. One of my new friends—I'll call him Bixby—loved to make fun of how I spoke. Bixby did not seem to be aware that making fun of my British African accent during classes was very painful for me. I tried to explain to him, but he didn't listen. Finally, I went to the head of the program, who simply told him to stop. This was another in a series of painful incidents that illustrated to me the depth of racism in this country.

Exercise on Separation and Selfhood

1. As we have shared our stories of growing up, perhaps you, too, are becoming aware of the pressures that we all receive as young people longing to belong and be a part of a whole. So often, the way a particular group comes together is through defining itself in contrast to groups that are considered the "other." Many times we are not aware of how racism has shaped our lives. Take a few minutes to reflect on any experiences you may have had that have shaped how you viewed yourself or the "other." Do you find yourself wondering: Who am I really?

2. Ask yourself: What decisions did I make in my early adulthood that shaped how I see myself racially? Consider any direct experiences with racism from this period of your life.

3. Take a few minutes and focus on the following questions. After each question, take a moment to close your eyes and breathe deeply. Then review the answers that come to you.

Who Am I?

- Who am I with regard to my racial identity?
- Who am I with regard to my race in the workplace?
- Who am I with regard to my race in the community I live in?
- Who am I with regard to my race in relation to my mate, my home, my family, and my friends?

4. After you reflect on your sense of who you are racially, consider the following questions:

- How deep were the roots of racism during your young adulthood?
- During your young adulthood, did you think that direct actions, government programs, or a new technology might solve racism? Were you even aware of racism as a problem?
- As you reexamine your own deeply held assumptions with regard to intolerance, did you ever think as a young adult that the system needed to be changed? If so, did you experience resistance?
- Did it ever occur to you that there is another way?

5. As you review the answers that surface, take a moment and let all the thoughts go. Now, how do you feel? See what comes to you when you look deeper. How willing are you to risk a deeper look where perhaps there are no words or forms? This is where true healing begins. To be part of a collective mind involves embarking on this healing journey, which requires a change of heart at a deep level. As you honestly face your answers to the questions posed here, you are becoming part of the healing process for all of humanity.

CHAPTER THREE

The Path to Love

*The universe, which is not merely the stars
and the moon and the planets, flowers, grass, and trees,
but all the people, has evolved no terms for your existence,
has made no room for you, and if love will not swing
wide the gates, no other power will or can.*

JAMES BALDWIN

The pain that racism causes can provide a stepping-stone for our personal growth, and our individual work can create major shifts in the larger social context, so that our children will not have to learn through pain, fear, and rejection. We decided on love as our learning tool, and the truth of the adage "You teach what you want to learn" came to life for us. This perspective became an active process affecting everything we did and operating with everyone we met.

This chapter tells how love opened wide the gates of choice for us. As we have followed the path of our healing, we have learned that *we can choose to see differently.* Prejudices and biases that we learned over the years can be unlearned. This is not an easy process, but we believe that through support and willingness we can shift the way we see ourselves and others. Our journey has taught us about the power of choice and the truth that we can always choose again.

In this chapter we will describe the beginning of the transformational process of both writers and how we began our personal healing journeys. As you read our stories, you might reflect on moments of opening and deeper awareness in your own life.

The Miracle Arrives

In the previous chapter, I (Aeeshah) described my experience as a Black Muslim. During that time, I believed that only some of the people on earth were children of God. I felt it was necessary to separate myself from those who were un-Godlike, and I had no idea that with this attitude I was limiting myself from experiencing the totality of God's presence. I believed that if God had wanted everyone to be brothers and sisters, and experience human kinship, God would have included all people in the African ethnicity.

I had an enormous amount of love in my heart; however, it was only shared with a portion of people on earth, and I added to my confusion by teaching this lesson to others. I taught love *and* fear. I told my people that whites were to be feared and hated because they were not children of God due to the color of their skin and the historical misdeeds of their ancestors. As a result, *my* experiences of the people of this earth were mixed with love and fear, and I did not experience the totality of God's love.

You may wonder how I came out of this confused state of mind. I did not do it alone. I was helped by my internal teacher, whom I sometimes refer to as the Holy Spirit.

While on my path of spiritual confusion, I would experience moments when I sensed an inner urge to know more and be more than what had been shown me thus far. Books would come to me that were unrelated to my chosen path—books that spoke of another path which dealt with the concept of the oneness of God. These books stirred within me a longing that I was not fully capable of fulfilling. My desire to be at one with God was like a tiny light in a dark room, and I began to question my belief system. I wondered to myself: What does it mean for society if all white people are devils? How can there be a oneness of God if some are excluded? The more I opened myself to experiencing this oneness, the more I perceived within my chosen path a weakness that could not withstand the test of reason.

One day, in a moment of inner turmoil, I asked: If there is a oneness in God, how can I experience it? No sooner had I asked this question than an answer came to me. It was a Sunday afternoon, and I was reading the *Oakland Tribune*. On the front page of one section was an article announcing a parapsychological seminar to be held at a nearby university. As I read the article, a voice from within me clearly told me that I was to attend this seminar. I was puzzled because I had never before felt an inner voice with such clarity. While I concentrated on what had transpired, I again heard, "Go!"

The following morning, I telephoned the institution where the seminar was to be held. I spoke with the secretary, who immediately referred me to the director of the program. I introduced myself and requested an appointment with him. He said that he would be pleased to meet with me, and we made an appointment for the following afternoon.

I arrived feeling a bit apprehensive about my reason for being there, and I went into the administrative office simply to get the appointment over with. The secretary informed me that the director was expecting me, and took me into his office. I sat there wondering what this man thought of me. Did he think I was crazy because my manner of dressing wasn't acceptable in the wider society? Did he wonder why this

Black Muslim would come to see him? All kinds of thoughts ran through my mind. As I sat in a chair directly in front of him, he was very patient as I fumbled through my purse to get the news clipping about the parapsychological seminar. "How may I help you?" he asked very quietly. I began talking nonstop about my chosen spiritual path, telling him that I had been guided to attend this conference, and asked if it was possible for me to come. I added that I did not have any money and I knew that there was a fee to attend.

He listened very attentively, nodding his head as if he understood. Then he said, "You can attend, but you will have to agree to pay the fee at a later date." I agreed and left his office feeling a sense of accomplishment.

The following Sunday I found myself seated in a large auditorium filled with white people, whom I had been taught to fear and hate, and to be suspicious of, because they were un-Godlike. I moved forward to the front row so that the population I was in the midst of would not preoccupy my mind. I sat down and pulled my hat over my forehead so that my eyes would be shaded, and I folded my arms as a sign that I was on guard.

The day began with parapsychologists presenting information intended to bridge the gap between psychology and spirituality. Their presentations were informative but dull. Finally, a woman named Judith Skutch came to the podium. She was introducing a set of books entitled *A Course in Miracles.* She began her talk by reciting the introduction. It goes like this: "This is a course in miracles. It is a required course. Only the time you take it is voluntary. Free will does not mean that you can establish the curriculum. It means only that you can elect what you want to take at a given time. The course does not aim at teaching the meaning of love, for that is beyond what can be taught. It does aim, however, at removing the blocks to the awareness of love's presence, which is your natural inheritance. The opposite of love is fear, but what is all-encompassing can have no opposite. The course can therefore be summed up very simply in this way: Nothing real can be threatened. Nothing unreal exists. Herein lies the peace of God."

As she said these words, I became one with them, time stopped, and there was a long period of silence. I heard deep within me an inner voice, which told me, "This is a tool for you, dear child. Use it, and I will guide your way. For I am with you always." The woman at the podium began to glow, and I heard the inner voice add, "This is your sister, whom I love dearly." I was filled with love in my heart for this woman. I also felt at home and safe. This was a very strange experience for me because this woman was from among those very people whom I believed were un-Godlike. Yet a voice deep within me spoke of God's love for her. I sat quietly after her presentation, thinking about what had transpired. I no longer could base my separatist belief on anything I felt, because all I felt at that moment was unconditional love for all of the children on the earth. At that moment, God's love entered my heart and dispelled any false belief I had held about any of the earth's people.

It wasn't easy to sustain this transcended perception about my surroundings, and I began to feel doubt about my feeling of oneness. I felt good inside, but I still wasn't sure if I should be experiencing love without measuring and evaluating. "Were these books necessary?" was a question that persisted in my consciousness. Why should I trust this one experience as a valid reason to purchase a set of books I had never examined closely?

I sat in my seat for a prolonged period, observing people moving toward the back of the auditorium to purchase books from a man who was smiling and being very polite. On a conscious level, I felt that it would be a wild goose chase to buy these books with the idea that they would serve some useful purpose in my spiritual process. I looked at all the people in the auditorium and judged against them. Then I slowly walked to the back of the room to inquire about the cost of the books. The man there informed me in an unusually warm manner that they had sold all the books on hand. I felt relieved and thought that this was a sign that I wasn't supposed to have them. Just as I was about to turn away, the man told me that his name was Jerry Jampolsky, and if I wanted the books I could come to a meeting at his home on Thursday evening. He proceeded to give me the directions I would need. I will be very honest. I was suspicious and fearful of his overly friendly manner. I left the seminar feeling very confused about my chosen spiritual path. I also felt a sense of being comforted by a still, small voice saying, "Be still, my child, and know that I am with you always."

At that time, my circle of friends and supporters consisted of others who embraced the same thought system as myself. I wondered with whom I could possibly share this experience. How could I tell them that I wanted to go to the home of someone we felt must be avoided so that we would not be deceived? I knew I did not want to go alone, but I did want to go. As I pondered my situation, again, for only a moment, I heard a still voice saying, "Don't worry about who shall go, for that is already taken care of." I relaxed and made a choice not to rebuke this voice.

The next day my dear friend Sharifah called to inquire about the parapsychological seminar. I shared with her my interest in

A Course in Miracles, and said I wanted to purchase the books, but I would have to go to the overwhelmingly white community of Tiburon on Thursday evening. She was interested but unsure about going. I shared with her that I did not really want anyone else to know because we would have to be among people who were not children of God. When she heard this, she decided that she could not possibly let me go alone.

I had met Sharifah in the Nation of Islam. She embodied the essence of sisterhood that the women involved in the Nation aspired to. One of the sayings of Muslim women was "Always want for your sister what you want for yourself, and love your sister as yourself." Sharifah was an extraordinary visionary, artist, and teacher who had grown up in Oakland. She had told me that although she was a Black Muslim woman, she had always felt comfortable with white people. She had jokingly shared with me how her father used to move to someplace new whenever too many black people moved into their neighborhood.

Sharifah told me that her best friend when she was five years old was a little white girl who lived next door to her. She went on to describe the first time she spent the night at her house. They were taking their baths after a long day of play and fun. Her friend turned to her and asked her why her skin did not come clean when she took her bath. That was the first time she was aware of being made to feel different.

As I think back to that time in my life, I realize that Sharifah was the perfect person to accompany me on my journey toward a shift in perception. She had the uncanny ability to support almost anyone, and she did so unconditionally.

I spent the rest of the week wrestling with my split mind. Was I crazy? Here I was wanting to go into the midst of beings whom I thought diabolical. Why was I planning to go?

To get a set of books that voice inside me insisted would guide me home. All of this did not really make any sense. But I knew that I would go.

On Thursday evening, my friend and I arrived in Tiburon. Jerry Jampolsky lived in a beautiful duplex apartment situated on a cliff overlooking the San Francisco Bay. While we parked, it was clear to us that this neighborhood was well cared for. The surrounding lawns were carefully manicured, and it was obvious that they were maintained by professionals. "How beautiful they are," I thought to myself. I have always loved beautiful grounds that are adorned with flowers and trees. It was very different from West Oakland, where trees were sparse and most lawns were maintained by the people who lived there, or not at all.

As we entered the house, Jerry greeted us with a warm smile. Of course, I was suspicious of his warm regard for me. His home was filled with people, all of whom were classified by me as Satan's children. I saw myself as separate from everyone in the room except for my friend, Sharifah; however, the room was very crowded, and we were forced to separate. I found myself sitting quietly between two strange bodies that were unlike mine.

Once we were seated, our first instruction was to hold hands and sense our inherent connectedness. I sat there looking first to my left, then to my right, thinking, "I could never hold those hands." I noticed that the people next to me were looking puzzled, and I was feeling uncomfortable. Then I heard Jerry say, "Can we all hold hands and join?" I was thinking, "Join?" This was not my idea of joining. I slowly stretched forth my hands to the two people on either side of me. I closed my mind to blot out the presence of their white bodies. My mind was active with fearful thoughts—fear of the past, fear of oppression and racial strife, and fear that the children of God *were* connected and not separate.

I felt the grasp of their hands over mine. Then, as I began to breathe deeply, relaxing in the environment I was in, for a moment I began to feel loved and safe. And I was, to my surprise, sending love out to the people who were next to me, and I could sense this loving energy moving out to everyone in that room. Again I heard a voice deep within me: "My child, teach only love, for this is what you are." I felt safe and at home. At that moment, I knew that everyone in the room was my brother or sister, and I was one with each one of them. As I opened my eyes, the bodies I had perceived as enemies were transformed into friends and loved ones.

I must be very honest right here. I by no means had reached a state of total unconditional love for everyone. I had not even reached a state of partial unconditional love. These were simply the first glimpses of what I might hope to experience in a peaceful state of mind—a goal to aspire to and strive for.

In the following months, I continued to ask questions about the impact of the separatist teachings I had been following. What was their effect on the world? I asked myself how I could truly make the world a better place for all people. Over time, I became an active volunteer at Jerry Jampolsky's Center for Attitudinal Healing. In those days, the center was located in Tiburon, California, which meant that its clientele was predominantly white. Its staff, up to that point, was all white. At this phase of my life, the center in Tiburon represented the "other." The principles of attitudinal healing challenged me to apply them indiscriminately to everyone I met. I took action and began the process of letting go of the separatist teachings I had taken within me.

As I studied the principles of attitudinal healing and made them mine by experimenting with them and putting them into practice in my life, I was surprised to find that I began to experience trust and was able to share my feelings in an atmosphere of nonjudgmental acceptance. I found these principles to be essential in my personal transformation. They have empowered me to choose peace in environments that would ordinarily be very difficult.

Through this work, I began to see the value in teaching what I want to learn. I began to get in touch with a concept that my mother had taught to me and all her children. She had taught us that our essence was love, and she had given love to us unconditionally. I recall my mother flying to California for the specific purpose of visiting the mosque I was attending. She accompanied me to the mosque, even though she felt strongly that this was not the path that "her Jesus" walked. She later told me that she endured the humiliation of her body being searched, which the women had to go through in order to enter the temple, because she loved me and needed to know for herself how and where I had chosen to serve. I remember her saying to me that Sunday, "I came because I had to see for myself what you have chosen." She always claimed that I was her baby and she had allowed me to leave home too soon, before I had fully developed.

Now, as I began my study of *A Course in Miracles*, I began to reclaim our original and most natural inheritance, love. The *Course* and the service work I began performing at the Center for Attitudinal Healing in Tiburon was essential in my shift from fear to love. The study of the principles, and my service work grounded in these principles, provided a theoretical and a practical means for the personal work that I had to do to begin the healing of the wounds of racism. My experience demonstrates that we can begin to let go of our painful historical past, even as it relates to the deepest wounds of racism, and we can share our healing with others.

Kokomon's Story Continues

As I described in the last chapter, my time in the United States had exposed me to racism in a profound and personal way. All that I had absorbed from my upbringing as a Christian and all of my understanding of brotherhood and sisterhood from my African perspective were shattered as a result of my negative experiences of racism.

As I continued my exploration of spirituality, I became involved with a wonderful woman who was Mexican American. I had met her while I was touring with my band in Los Angeles. Friendship ensued, and eventually we became engaged to be married. We planned a Buddhist ceremony. For the second time I experienced racism on my wedding day. My fiancé's family, in an attempt to stop our marriage, decided to boycott the wedding. My fiancé could not believe that her family, with whom she had always been close, would reject her in this way simply because I was a black man. I was ready to call the wedding off; it was so painful to go through this again. But my fiancé wanted to go ahead with our plans. So we got married without her family in attendance. The wedding was a small and peaceful gathering, with a Buddhist ceremony attended by fellow students from the Temple of Esoteric Sciences, a Buddhist temple and school.

Studying Buddhism at the Temple of Esoteric Sciences was an important part of my spiritual and healing process. My wife and I studied meditation and Eastern philosophy. I learned to see the world not as a collection of physical objects but as a complicated web of relations between the various parts of a unified whole. I was very familiar with this concept, because in my African culture the Ga people of Ghana had imparted a similar message. For example, the African saying "It takes a village to raise a child" reflects the sense of kinship I had experienced from a very early age—a sense of connection to the whole human family.

One day a friend invited my wife and me to attend the Church of Religious Sciences on Wilshire Boulevard in Los Angeles. Minister William Honaday gave a sermon on love and law. After the service, we learned that Dr. Honaday was starting a class on the Science of Mind. The Science of Mind is the teaching that the great love of the universe must be one with the great law of its own being, and we approach love through the law. The founder, Ernest Holmes, has stated that the hardest thing for human beings to do is to know themselves and change themselves. "There is but Unity; there is nothing but Totality. It is like the sunlight of Eternal Truth bursting through the clouds of obscurity and bathing all of life in a celestial glory. It is the Absolute with which we are dealing and nothing less."

As I struggled with the negative effects of racism, I found the teachings of Ernest Holmes very helpful, providing an important prescription for my dilemma. I also participated in meetings at the Self-Realization Fellowship, where I absorbed the teachings of Paramahansa Yogananda.

Lord, may Thy love shine forever
on the sanctuary of my devotion,
and may I be able to awaken Thy love in all hearts.

PARAMAHANSA YOGANANDA

Time passed, and my marriage of twelve years broke up in 1990. At that point, I moved from Los Angeles back to the Bay Area and settled in Oakland. I wasn't sure why I needed to be back in Oakland, but somehow I sensed that it was connected to expressing my artistic and musical talents to help transform and heal humanity. On my return to Oakland, I reconnected with Aeeshah.

Aeeshah and I had originally met in 1977. I had just arrived in Oakland, California, to work with the popular West African musical group Hedzoleh Soundz. During that time, the manager of the group had organized a West African Cultural Center to educate the community about the Ghanaian culture. We taught Ga language classes two times a week, and Aeeshah had attended one of them. I was immediately attracted to her and asked her over for dinner. I wanted to cook some African food for her. She accepted my invitation. I remember being quite excited. I prepared ground nut stew with rice and fried plantain. When Aeeshah arrived, she had five children with her. I wondered if all these children were hers. She introduced me to them, and I discovered that two were hers: a five-year-old girl named Amanah and a nineteen-month-old boy named Imam. The other children were her friends: Nadirah, age seven, Tahirah, age five, and Sherod, age three. Aeeshah was polite enough. I learned that she was a Black Muslim, but not entirely, because she had begun to explore a thought system that posed some serious questions for her. She also shared that she was separated from the children's father.

We all ate dinner, and as soon as dinner was over, Aeeshah announced that she had to leave because she had to get the children home since their bedtime was 8:30 P.M. It was then 8:15, and I watched as she packed the children up one by one and left promptly. I stood there in my little house with dirty dishes from feeding six people. I wondered about this woman who seemed so wrapped up in her community. As it turned out, Aeeshah and I were to go our separate ways. She married an African from our community, and I moved to Los Angeles, where I met the Mexican American woman I was married to for twelve years.

Now, twelve years later, Aeeshah and I were again spending time together. One day I was talking with her, and she shared with me her dream of creating a tape of spiritual poetry with African rhythms as the background music. The pieces she had chosen were from *The Gifts of God,* written by Helen Schucman, the scribe of *A Course in Miracles.* She needed someone who could write original pieces for each poem. So that I would understand the poems in depth, Aeeshah suggested I watch a film entitled *A Course in Miracles.* I watched the film and found it to be very profound. I started reading the set of books, and I also joined a study group that met every Sunday afternoon in West Oakland to read and share the concepts of *A Course in Miracles.*

Aeeshah and I began to work together on *The Gifts of God* project with the support of the Foundation of Inner Peace, a nonprofit organization whose mission was to publish and disseminate *A Course in Miracles* and other *Course*-related material written by Helen Schucman. As Aeeshah and I worked together, our relationship grew, and our desire for a holy relationship blossomed into marriage in 1994. We have been very grateful for the opportunity to join and share our lives.

During the time I was reconnecting with Aeeshah, I started practicing the daily lessons in the *Course,* which provided a final realization to my search. The teachings in *A Course of Miracles* reached to the core of my being and helped me resolve the most problematic issue I was faced with—racism. As Ernest Holmes eloquently stated:

The Circle Is Complete

The Circle of Love is complete.
It comprehends all, includes all, and binds together
with cords of Everlasting Unity.
I cannot depart from Its Presence nor wander from Its care.
My love is complete within me.
The Love of God binds me to Itself, and will not let me go.
I shall make a home for you, O my wonderful Love,
and we shall journey through life hand in hand.

ERNEST HOLMES

Out of this understanding, I feel obligated to share my freedom with my brothers and sisters—the medicine to cure the catastrophic disease which President Clinton has called "a curse on America"—racism.

Exercise on Opening to Healing

Healing comes in many different forms. In telling you our stories, we have explored some of the painful messages we received about race, leading to a sense of separation and sometimes despair. In this chapter, both of us have also shared with you some of the key experiences on our path to healing. Wherever you may find yourself on your own unique path, we hope our experiences will remind you of some of the messages and gifts you have received in your own life that point toward hope and the possibility of true healing.

1. Allow yourself to remember a moment in your life when you gained a special insight into your connection with someone you at first viewed as totally different from yourself. If you can't remember anything specific, let yourself imagine what it would be like to experience such an insight.

2. Sit quietly and let your breathing deepen. Consider the possibility that you are reading this book because you are meant to be a part of the healing of the planet around racial separation. You wouldn't even have opened the pages unless some part of you were ready to take the next step. Healing is a process, not a goal. You don't have to do it all at once. All you have to do is find the courage to take the next step. The principles of attitudinal healing described in Part Two will offer you many keys. Once you become aware, opportunities to contribute to racial healing will present themselves to you quite naturally.

Twelve Spiritual Keys to Racial Healing

The Principles of Attitudinal Healing

Love is like whisky,
Like sweet red wine
If you want to be happy
You got to love all the time.

LANGSTON HUGHES

In Part Two, we will share with you the most effective means we know for breaking through the deeply internalized racism dwelling in all of us. Our primary goal is focused on us as individuals, and as a society, developing the emotional capacity to accept and love all of humanity. We know that loving all of humanity is an awesome task, and we know that we could never have embarked on this journey without spiritual help. This process of spiritual connection has enabled us to share our experiences with you.

The principles of attitudinal healing—which flow from core teachings in the seminal text *A Course in Miracles* and in Dr. Gerald (Jerry) Jampolsky's and Dr. Diane Cirincione's work—provide keys for resolving the thorniest of issues. The principles of attitudinal healing, which express universal spiritual principles, can indeed help us heal the wounds of history, bring global healing, and provide a return to wholeness. When these principles are incorporated into our lives, they give a deep understanding of the problems facing humanity, and the ability to confront the disease of racism with surprising ease. They permit us to move beyond fear and experience healing in all our endeavors.

With the understanding and practice of these spiritual principles, we create *hedzoleh,* a word meaning peace and love in the Ga language of Ghana, West Africa. We put ourselves in harmony with nature. When we as individuals are at peace and in a state of joy, the global village will be joyous, and our national community will finally be at peace.

The journey toward racial healing does not entail a final destination. It is a lifelong process of letting go: letting go of our shame, our guilt, and our painful past so that we are free to experience fulfilling relationships, love, and happiness, first for ourselves, next for our families, our local communities, and our country, and finally for the world. As Deepak Chopra has stated, "In reality, we are divinity in disguise, and the gods and goddesses in embryo that are contained within us seek to be fully materialized." The unfolding of this divinity within us holds the promise of true racial healing.

Putting Spiritual Principles to Work

The principles of attitudinal healing flow out of the teachings of *A Course in Miracles,* a spiritual work exploring the dynamics of the ego and of our relationship with God. It is not necessary for you to be familiar with that text in order to benefit from these principles. Their truth becomes evident as you come to understand them and put them into practice in your life. Throughout Part Two, we will be referring to these twelve principles, sharing stories from our lives that illustrate them, and suggesting ways you might put them into effect in your own life to bring about racial healing.

The Principles of Attitudinal Healing

1. The essence of our being is love.

2. Health is inner peace, and healing is letting go of fear.

3. Giving and receiving are the same.

4. We can let go of the past and of the future.

5. Now is the only time there is, and each instant is for giving.

6. We can learn to love ourselves and others by forgiving rather than judging.

7. We can become love finders rather than fault finders.

8. We can choose and direct ourselves to be peaceful inside regardless of what is happening outside.

9. We are students and teachers to each other.

10. We can focus on the whole of life rather than the fragments.

11. Since love is eternal, death need not be viewed as fearful.

12. We can always perceive ourselves and others as either extending love or giving a call for help.

The Principles of Attitudinal Healing

Attitudinal healing stems from the belief that the purpose of all communication is joining, not separation. Attitudinal healing reflects the understanding that we are not only responsible for our thoughts, we are also responsible for the feelings we experience. Through exploring these feelings, and coming to terms with them, we can eventually heal them. This involves the process of letting go of painful, fearful attitudes about our experiences. Through this, we learn to choose love rather than fear, and peace rather than conflict. We learn how to forgive ourselves, and in forgiving ourselves we learn how to forgive others. Attitudinal healing helps us recognize that it is not people, places, or events that cause us to feel upset. What causes us pain are our thoughts, our guilt, and our judgments about people, experiences, and events. Attitudinal healing involves removing these inner obstacles to experiencing peace. When we let go of fear, only love remains.

As you read our stories In Part Two, and the stories of some of the courageous men and women who have shared their stories with us, you'll learn more about why we feel these principles are uniquely suited to helping us heal ourselves and the deep wounds caused by racism.

CHAPTER FOUR

Love Lives in Us All

It lives in all of us on a primordial level
inexplicable but undeniable.

MAYA ANGELOU

ATTITUDINAL HEALING PRINCIPLE #1

"The essence of our being is love."

Just saying these words—"The essence of our being is love"—is meaningless, but believing them is everything. Many times we think of love, but we seldom think of it as a totally inward process that flows outward once we believe and experience it. To believe that your essence is love is a process that involves embracing your entire being.

So often we think of love as something that is exclusive, such as loving "my" being, "my" family, "my" community. However, if you read the words of the first principle of attitudinal healing closely, you will realize that "The essence of our being is love" reflects a sense of joining or oneness. We are challenged to move past our old ways of thinking, in which we move through life with barriers and blocks to joining. Have you ever walked into a room and you were the only person there who was of your ethnicity and race? What did you experience? What were your perceptions? Were you able to move into an emotional space of acceptance? This is the challenge that this principle presents. Can we experience love as the essence of all beings as well that which connects us to all beings? Through love we are truly all one.

Love Lives in Us All

The time for the healing of the wounds has come.
The moment to bridge the chasms has come.

NELSON ROLIHLAHLA MANDELA
Inaugural speech

Love is looking beyond appearances, beyond personalities—
and beyond our perceptions of ourselves and others. The most
prevalent obstacle to the awareness of love is our own self-
doubt, our own feelings of unworthiness, of superiority or inferiority. This principle challenges us to explore and know the
truth that we can choose how we feel about ourselves and
others. Through the power of love, we can change our minds;
we can take the next step on our journey of racial healing.

Myrna's Story

The work we do facilitating Healing Racism workshops has
helped us to understand the complexities of racism as well as
the myriad of emotional layers associated with this issue. A
young woman named Myrna came to one of our Healing
Racism Circles. She was relieved to find a place to share her
pain. Her parents were immigrants from India, but Myrna was
born in the United States and raised in Concord, California.
When she first came to the circle, she spoke bitterly of her
painful youth. She said, "I have never been able to talk about
the racism I have experienced with my parents, because I did
not want to disturb them. They have tried to give me the best
that they felt this country had to offer." Myrna went on to say
that she had been reared in a predominantly white neighborhood and that this was the source of her pain.

At first glance, it is difficult to associate Myrna with any
race in particular. She could be a Mexican, Pakistani, Native

American, Iranian, or mulatto. Her skin tone is olive, her hair is jet black, and her eyes somewhat almond-shaped. Myrna told us, "Growing up in my community was extremely scary." She was frequently the recipient of racial stereotypes attributed to Mexicans, and when she would try to explain that she was not Mexican, other students did not believe her. Myrna said, "I was constantly teased and taunted by my classmates."

Myrna spoke of her high school years as the worst, because the assumptions placed on her were untrue. The level of hatred really got out of hand during the Iranian hostage crisis, when some Iranians held some Americans hostage. Myrna was attacked verbally and physically at school because some of the students thought she was Iranian and began to call her the enemy. The abuse got so bad that Myrna was stabbed with a knife, and cigarettes were put out on her hand. She was afraid to go to school.

Even after Myrna grew up and moved away from home, she still did not feel able to share her real feelings with her parents. She moved to San Francisco because it is one of the most multicultural cities in the country. In our Healing Racism Circle, Myrna chose to work with the first attitudinal healing principle, "The essence of our being is love," because she realized that the young people who had harmed her were not looking at her essence; they were looking at her apparent covering. She did not want to continue to replicate their mistakes. She wished that there had been a dialogue when she was in school with a group whose focus was racial healing. She feels that this would have saved her years of fear and anguish. She attended our Healing Racism Circle for almost a year and felt that these sessions were invaluable in helping her to get in touch with her wholeness. Myrna felt that joining with other people in the circle allowed her to move beyond the injuries of her youth and embrace the truth of who she is in the present. She felt layers of fear start to drop away. By sharing her story and hearing the stories of others in the circle, Myrna learned a new appreciation for her own being as part of the whole. In this way, we can remind one another that the essence of all of us is love.

PUTTING PRINCIPLE #1 INTO PRACTICE

"The essence of our being is love."

1. In our ruggedly individualistic society, we are not trained to think in terms of the whole. However, we can begin to practice holding this way of thinking in our consciousness. To deepen your experience of these words, stop everything that you are doing—stop even analyzing these words—and practice the following steps.

2. Sit quietly, and take three long, deep breaths. Close your eyes, and picture a Native American family, an East Indian family, a white family, a black family, and a mixed race family.

3. Now, very slowly, say to yourself, "The essence of our being is love." Allow yourself to accept this statement totally. Rest with the words, noticing any resistance that you may feel. Breathe slowly, allowing yourself to be with any resistance you experience, while embracing the people you are holding in your mind.

4. If any feelings of fear or anxiety should surface, say to yourself slowly: "When we let go of fear, only love remains. Letting go of fear is the avenue by which we

begin to heal our mind." When we are not feeling harmonious with ourselves and others, when we do not see the love in others, we are experiencing symptoms of separation. Whenever we find ourselves judging others in any way, we are not sensing them as they are, and this will lead to worry, anxiety, and a loss of peace. In such cases, you can always stop, take a long, deep breath, and say to yourself slowly, "The essence of our being is love."

CHAPTER FIVE

Letting Go of Fear

*Your pain is the breaking of the shell
that encloses your understanding.*

KAHLIL GIBRAN

ATTITUDINAL HEALING PRINCIPLE #2

*"Health is inner peace,
and healing is letting go of fear."*

As we have looked deeply into the pain of racism over the years, we have come to realize again and again that we could never heal these awesome wounds without some kind of spiritual support. We have seen through the years that we can deal with blatant discrimination through legal channels and receive some corrective action, but these kinds of compensation cannot heal hearts. Our goal is deeper healing, and this requires spiritual as well as practical and supportive processes. We want nothing less than total release from the pain and fear that racist conditioning breeds. This means looking deeply into the part we all play in keeping the separation alive.

We ask you to walk with us as we describe how we began to move through our fears. In our own lives, the principles of attitudinal healing proved invaluable to this process. Saying to ourselves, "Health is inner peace, and healing is letting go of fear," offers us an important step along the path to healing. To truly start to live this basic principle takes us to the next level—that of actualization in our world.

Sometimes we fear that if we forgive someone we perceive has wronged us, our forgiveness will let the "bad guy" get away with it. We are afraid to trust the law of compensation (sometimes called the law of karma, or the law of cause and effect) to work on the worldly plane, but our task does not include judging our co-workers, our neighbors, or those we think have wronged us. Our task rather lies in loving ourselves unconditionally and extending that unconditional love out to all we meet. Healing our mind of racial overtones in a society that was formed out of the fabric of racial categorization poses a challenge. However, as we rise to meet this challenge, this practice frees us from the world of conflict and fear.

Transforming Fear to Peace

Not too long ago, I (Kokomon) worked for a delivery company as a courier. It was the month of December, and I had on a coat to protect me from the cold. I went to Lake Merritt Plaza to deliver a package to a business on the twenty-fourth floor of a large building. I entered the elevator, and while I was waiting for it to take off, a young white woman walked in. As soon as she was in, the door closed and the elevator took off. She was also going to the twenty-fourth floor. Just as she was about to press the button, she realized the light was already on.

At this point, she registered that there was somebody else in the elevator and that this person happened to be a black man — me. Fear came over her; it was palpable. I could tell she was very, very afraid of me. She was an attractive woman dressed in black, wearing some type of coat over a black mini-skirt.

Because I could sense her fear, I took a position as far away from her as I could. The inside of the elevator ceiling was decorated with a mirror, so I could look at her just by glancing at the ceiling. She had her head down, and she was in her corner, and I was in mine. All kinds of thoughts were going through my head, because I had been reading stories regarding the lynching of black men in America who for one reason or another had been accused of raping white women. When I sensed that she was afraid—she was actually trembling with fear—I got alarmed. I became very frightened myself. What if this woman were to level an accusation against me? How would I defend myself? This was very disturbing. I focused on the elevator panel and the signs of progress from floor to floor. I could feel my own fear growing.

Then, I realized that I could do something to help me let go of my growing fear. I could make a different choice. I took a deep breath and started repeating to myself a prayer to acknowledge that my spirit and the woman's spirit were one, that we had one mind, and that that mind was one of love and kindness and nothing else. I transmitted the idea that I had no interest in who she was other than to respect her as a woman and a human being—that I did not know her, I didn't want money from her, and I had no interest whatsoever.

I found it amazing that by the time the elevator was passing the eighteenth floor, she was getting the message—by mental telepathy, by love, by whatever you want to call it—that we just happened to be in the same elevator at the same time, and that's it. I noticed that her energy was changing. I could see in the mirror in the ceiling that she was beginning to look at me, and she could see that I was on some important mission, and that she just happened to be in the elevator. She turned to me, and greeted me. All of a sudden she said out loud, "I am no longer afraid of you." I took a deep breath and turned to her. I wanted to ask her why she'd been afraid of me. I was very shaken by the whole experience, as she validated my perception of her fear. What could have caused that fear, other than the fact that I was a black man? I didn't know her.

This is the work of prejudice, I thought to myself. Prejudice is an unfavorable opinion or feeling that is formed beforehand. Because of her preconceptions, this woman feared me for no other reason than that I was a black man. When she said, "I am no longer afraid of you," I wanted to ask a million questions. Had she been offended by a black person or a black man before? Had she had any altercation with a black person? What information had she picked up from the media? But I was tongue-tied, and I was also on my job, so when the elevator reached the twenty-fourth floor we parted, and I went about my business.

The experience stuck with me, though, revealing both the fear that prejudice leads to, and the healing power of loving thoughts.

Inner Peace and True Health

Most of the time when we think of health, we think of our physical body. However, our focus in this book is about our mind and our great need for inner peace, which leads to racial healing. Mother Teresa, who worked so devotedly during her lifetime to uplift the poor and diseased, said that the most serious problem facing us in the twentieth century is spiritual deprivation.

We are inclined to resonate with this belief, and for this reason we have defined racism as a life-threatening illness, a deprivation of the spirit. We have learned that racial harmony cannot be legislated. It is not a legal issue. It is a heart issue. Today more than ever we are torn emotionally over the issue of race. From the perspective of attitudinal healing, health is not about our physical condition; instead, health is seen as a state of being free of fear—a mental state. Health is a state of being free of conflict, free of emotional pain, free of guilt. Health is a harmonious state—alive, energetic, loving, and kind. In this state, we can experience a personal transformation. This is what true health is. You may be asking yourself right now: How can I experience this? Our belief is that you experience health by letting go of fear and setting a single goal of experiencing inner peace. You learn to let go of fear every time you intentionally keep your heart open at the very moment that you most feel like contracting. By breathing into the area in your chest that starts to constrict when you are afraid, you are choosing health and healing over fear and separation.

PUTTING PRINCIPLE #2 INTO PRACTICE

"Health is inner peace, and healing is letting go of fear."

1. We have been working with the principles of attitudinal healing for some time, and we still find that we struggle with them, especially when we are challenged with an opportunity to let go of our fears about the "other." None of us wants to admit that we may be feeling guilty or victimized, or that we may be acting as an oppressor when confronted with racial, cultural, class, or gender issues. And, let's face it, when we are experiencing fear, we cannot feel peaceful; we cannot experience true health. The key factor when we are faced with a fearful belief is to make the choice not to resist the feeling. We can admit to ourselves that we are not

peaceful and ask for help and express our fears and prejudices honestly. We have learned that it is often difficult to resolve these kinds of issues alone. The quickest way to let go of fear is to reach out to another human being. Many times we are experiencing so much embarrassment with issues related to racism that we are unable to ask for help. We bury our feelings. Simply reaching out to a friend or family member we trust can help us begin to change this dynamic.

2. However, if you find yourself experiencing the constriction of fear around the issue of race and you are not able to reach out to another, sit down quietly and do the following:

- Take a pen and paper and begin to list all your fearful thoughts about race. These might include your fears of the "other," as well as your fears about your own prejudice.

- Take several long, deep breaths as you list your fears, imagining yourself breathing the fears out as you list them.

- Then, make a contrasting list of loving images and breathe deeply. As you take these deep breaths, imagine yourself breathing in all the love from your positive images.

3. Remember, letting your breath flow and keeping your chest open allows you to let go of fear, and letting go of fear will bring you the true health of inner peace.

CHAPTER SIX

Giving and Receiving

To most of us society shows not its face and eye,
but its side and back. To stand in true relations with
[humanity] in a false age is worth a fit of insanity, is it not?

RALPH WALDO EMERSON

ATTITUDINAL HEALING PRINCIPLE #3

"Giving and receiving are the same."

This chapter focuses on trust and our ability to know deeply that trust is built on our willingness to question all the beliefs that hold us separate from other people. We hope to explore with you our challenges and how we overcame them. By going beyond our innermost fears and trusting the process, we reached a place of unconditional love. We can always focus on form and what distinguishes us from others, and race is sometimes the most obvious difference.

Fearful beliefs such as racial stereotypes are very powerful and very seductive, and we can almost always find one incident to cite that seems to validate or justify our belief. Such beliefs are deeply charged with painful emotion, and therefore are hard to examine closely. Most of us would rather not look. We're afraid to look at our prejudices because all too often we believe them, even if we don't think we should. However, each day we can become aware of our part in the great circle of giving and receiving, reminding us of our essential equality and helping us move beyond our prejudice.

The Beggar at BART

Every day, we are offered wonderful lessons to help us deepen our understanding of basic spiritual principles, all of which can be applied to healing racism. I (Aeeshah) had this experience some time ago. I used to ride on BART (Bay Area Rapid Transit) every day to get to work, and each time I'd approach the station there was always the same man sitting there begging. I never bothered to really look at him; I just rushed past like everyone else. Inside I was thinking: Please don't look at me, because I'm not going to give you a dime! Every morning when I left for work, he would be there, and every evening when I came home he would still be there.

At the time, it cost sixty cents for me to take the BART from 20th Street downtown to the West Oakland BART station, near where I lived. And one day, I got to the BART station to get out my sixty cents for a ticket, and all I could scrape together was fifty cents. I was digging and digging through my purse, but I couldn't seem to find one more dime.

I looked around, and everybody was in a hurry, trying to get home because it was the end of a long day. They were looking at me with the message to get out of the way. As I looked around, I was trying to make eye contact to see who might give me a dime. And as I looked, people avoided eye contact, with the unspoken message: Don't ask me! I almost felt like laughing, it was so absurd. Where was I ever going to get a dime?

I was starting to feel a little frantic. I turned around, and who was smiling at me? The same beggar I passed every morning and every evening. I went over to him rather sheepishly because I'd never really looked at him before, and I'd never spoken to him. "Hi!" I said.

92

He looked back at me with a happy expression and answered, "Hi! How you doin'?"

I told him that tonight I had a little problem. I said I needed a dime to get home on BART. "Um, could you lend me a dime?"

And he responded, "Sure, here's a quarter. Take a quarter!"

I said, "Look, all I need is a dime."

He said, "Come, take the quarter."

I looked at him with great relief, and I took the quarter and thanked him profusely. Then the social worker in me came to the surface, and I asked him his name. "Robert," he told me, and I asked him where he lived and whether he had board and care. I told him about the treatment center where I work and said that if he wanted to learn some skills he could come there and get some structure.

He looked at me and said, "I'm quite happy, thank you."

"But you're here at a BART station," I said.

Robert looked back at me and said, "Look, I meet all kinds of people here, and I really enjoy myself, and I don't want to change it."

So I thanked him again and got on BART, and as I was sitting there riding back home, I realized that I saw this man at the station every day, and what he was really doing was giving and receiving love. In my smallmindedness, I had only seen a beggar, but when I looked back on my experience with Robert, I realized that he had long since mastered the principle that giving and receiving are the same.

Giving and Getting: The Essential Flow of Life

For most of us, whenever we give we are secretly wondering what we will get. We measure and mete out everything, never allowing ourselves to relax with the ebb and flow of life, fearing that somehow if we give, we will lose.

What might be helpful is to begin to look at this process differently. Most of the time we think of form instead of content. When we think of giving and receiving, we are looking at what we will get and what we will give in terms of material things. From an attitudinal healing perspective, we are challenged to shift the way we perceive giving and receiving. We are asked to think of giving and receiving in terms of giving love and receiving love. In this ultimate sense, to give is truly to receive; what we put out we get back; and what we sow we also reap. All that we give is given to ourselves.

Life is a mirror. From the moment of our birth, giving and receiving are essential to our well-being. Focusing on giving and receiving simultaneously creates horizontally equal relationships in which all parts involved are valued equally. If you give without being open to receiving, you situate yourself in the position of higher rank—somehow better than the person you have given to. You rob that person of the joy of giving and the ability to help others. You create a vertical process in relationship to people and things around you. You are either above or below. Both positions tend to create guilt and the mode of being superior or inferior; this vertical dynamic is based on a sense of lack rather than abundance.

Reflect on this quote from Ralph Waldo Emerson:

The world looks like a multiplication-table,
or a mathematical equation, which, turn it how you will,
balances itself. Take what figure you will,
its exact value, not more nor less, still returns to you.
Every secret is told, every crime is punished, every virtue
rewarded, every wrong redressed, in silence and certainty.

What we call retribution is the universal necessity
by which the whole appears wherever a part appears.

RALPH WALDO EMERSON

PUTTING PRINCIPLE #3 INTO PRACTICE

"Giving and receiving are the same."

1. We are all giving and receiving at all times whether we are aware of it or not. The thoughts that you hold in your mind are being sent out and being returned to you moment by moment. This is true of your attitudes about race and racial differences. If you hold thoughts of lack, guilt, frustration, unworthiness, or judgment, these are the things that you will attract to yourself. This is the basis of giving and receiving. As we explore this principle, questions arise, such as:

- Do we give to receive?
- When we give should we or shouldn't we expect anything in return?
- Do we give what our loved ones want? Or, what we want for them?
- How can one measure the value of giving?
- Why are some of us afraid of receiving? Do we believe in a world that takes, because we believe that we can get by taking? If we give more to certain racial groups, do we fear that in so doing we might lose something we currently have?

2. The third attitudinal principle is powerful in healing relationships across cultural and other barriers. If practiced

seriously, this principle can help us free ourselves from feelings of loss related to giving. To internalize the tenet "Giving and receiving are the same," follow these simple steps:

- Whenever possible, when you visit a friend or a family, take a simple gift.

- Recognizing that your essence is love, agree to devote today to sharing your essence with everyone you encounter, whatever their racial, ethnic, or religious background.

- Agree to be an active participant in circulating joy, peace, love, and abundance with yourself and everyone in your life. The more you can give universally to the full rainbow spectrum of humanity, the more you will receive back.

- Practice being in a state of gratitude for all that you give and all that you receive. Reflect on the great gifts given by the wealth of diversity in the people who share this earth with you—from music, food, and art, to sports, entertainment, religion, philosophy, and science. Being in a state of gratitude opens the gates of grace, which is the most valuable gift that comes when one is grateful.

CHAPTER SEVEN

Letting Go of Past and Future

Dream softly of your sinless brother [and sister], who unites with you in holy innocence.

The answer that I give my brother [and sister] is what I am asking for.

A Course in Miracles

ATTITUDINAL HEALING PRINCIPLE #4

"We can let go of the past and of the future."

When we come to recognize that what we give to others is what we ourselves seek, we open the path to true healing. In order to stop the victimization, anger, and frustration of living in a society that is rooted in racism, it is important to come to the realization that when we give, we can only give to ourselves. We have some wonderful icons in our midst who demonstrate forgiveness, love, and living in the present for peace. Recently we had the honor to go to the Paramount Theater in Oakland to hear Coretta Scott King give a speech entitled "The Dream Deferred: Building Coalitions into the New Millennium." As soon as Mrs. King came on the stage, we could see that she walked the path of forgiveness. To speak on the theme of the dream deferred, even when your beloved was brutally murdered for that dream, requires a tremendous act of faith—the faith to keep on working on the dream without bitterness. Coretta Scott King mirrored for us the value and truth of living an attitudinally healed life of love and forgiveness. It is true that when we share love, happiness, and peace, we receive these qualities in our own lives. We have chosen to share why we value reaching out to others, going past our perceptions of differences. We share with you our experiences of going past form into content.

The Slave Castles of Ghana

Since I (Aeeshah) became exposed to the principles of attitudinal healing, I find myself making healing choices more and more, no matter what I'm faced with. But that doesn't mean I *always* make healing choices. Sometimes I am totally caught in ego: I feel self-righteous—I would rather be right than be happy—and I go about making sure that I am right. With this story I'm sharing with you, you'll see that even once you get on the path, it doesn't mean that you will always be totally in bliss and totally peaceful.

This experience happened when I traveled to Africa with my husband, Kokomon. It had always been my dream to return home and look on the place of departure of my ancestors. For this reason, I had changed my name many years before to Ababio. As fate would have it, I had married an African man in the 1970s whose last name was also Ababio. Ababio is a Ghanaian name from the Akan Tribe which means "one who has returned." On my trip to Africa, I was fulfilling my dream of returning and reclaiming my lost heritage.

During my first trip to Ghana, I intended to visit the slave castles as one part of exploring my people's history. Ghana is one of the smallest nations in Africa, but it has more than fifty slave prisons and dungeons, or slave castles, as they are called, built during the slave trade. These dungeons or castles are huge forts. Soon after we arrived in Ghana in 1992, we went to visit the Elmina Castle, which is one of the most famous castles.

Now, one of the most wonderful people I met in Ghana was Kofi Ghanabà, who lived in America in the 1950s. He is known in Ghana as "Odomankoma Kyrema," an Akan name which means "the divine drummer." He is a very powerful musician, and was very famous when he was in the United States. In 1956 he had released a hit album, "Africa Speaks, America Answers," which sold over a million copies.

As a very spiritual man, and an African shaman, Ghanabà was well aware of the African Holocaust—the atrocities of racism that killed millions of Africans during the hundreds of years of slave trade—and he had recently played the master drummer and medicine man in Hale Gerima's film *Sankofa*, an extremely powerful film about the African Holocaust. On the occasion of our visit in 1992, Ghanabà advised us, "Upon your visit to Elmina, spend some time in the town for a few days. Take yourselves around the outskirts of the castle first, and be sure to perform ablution. Ablutions provides a spiritual cleansing. Pray. Ask that your ancestors protect and guide you, and give you inner strength. And you, Aeeshah, in particular, take special care to perform this prayerful cleansing so that you will be able to embrace the emotional trauma of the atrocities committed in those dungeons."

But I ignored his advice. Other people had also warned me that African Americans almost always have past-life experiences when they go into these dungeons. But I thought of myself as the attitudinal healing queen, and I knew I was totally healed, so I wasn't worried. I thought I could go tour the dungeons and just deal with it and control my emotions.

As it happened, on the day we were to go to Elmina, I was vividly aware that I was the only African American on the tour. The castle itself was immense, as big as six city blocks, with a huge wall all around it. The walls were up to thirty feet high, with cannons on top. When we first walked inside the castle, we couldn't see the dungeon right away. We saw a large courtyard and other buildings. First we were taken to the old lieutenant's quarters, which is now an office. And then we moved to the governor's quarters. From the governor's quarters, which were built in the 1500s, we had an exotic view of little African red huts and colorful boats out on the ocean.

Then we went to the general store, and I began to realize that the castle was like a city within itself. It was truly a fort within a hostile land—a walled city to protect its precious cargo of slaves. As we continued the tour, we finally got back to ground level, where we could see some little doors, and one said "Slave Entrance." Everyone was entering that door. There were two Dutch men, a woman from England, and my Ghanaian husband among them. I was the last through the door, as I was taking pictures of everyone entering.

Once I got through the door to the dungeon, I saw over the left-hand corner a huge shrine with candles and sacred emblems. And as I began to walk in, I started hearing the voices of people screaming. "You are now walking on twelve inches of petrified human flesh and excrement," the guide was saying in the background. But I could hardly hear his voice because the cries of the screaming people who had died there were drowning it out.

I became petrified myself, and I doubled over into a fetal position on the floor of the dungeon castle. I began to sob big heaving sobs for the people who were screaming, crying to be released. In that moment, I no longer existed as Aeeshah; I had become one of the people who were screaming. I was one of the crying dead. I was trapped in this experience, with the stench of the dead; I was trapped there screaming.

I was finally aware of Kokomon beside me, helping me walk out. Everyone was ahead of us, and he was helping me move through the building, helping me through the experience. He actually picked me up and carried me through the experience. Once we were back in the courtyard and I stood up, I still didn't feel much like myself, as if I wasn't really in my body.

In the background, I could hear the two Dutch fellows talking, and they were talking about the beauty of the structure of the building and how well it was built. One of them was saying, "Can you believe it? This building is five hundred years old, and look how well it's built. Look at the structure; it's still intact!" And as I was standing there, I was one of the screaming dead. I looked over at them, and I don't know if they saw my eyes flaming or the smoke coming out of the top of my head. I looked at the man who had spoken, and I said, "How can you marvel at this structure when it holds such atrocity?"

I said this with great force, and the man looked over at me with disdain and anger and said, "You don't have to come here. You're not from here, and you don't have to come here." When he said this, I totally lost it. I became an angry, murderous person. I raced for his throat. I could practically feel his blood in my fingernails, but Kokomon was holding me back. I felt like killing this man. I felt murderous; I had no desire except to murder him. So at that point, attitudinal healing was out the window. I was not thinking that the essence of our being is love. I was not thinking about giving and receiving being one and the same. I was not thinking that I could choose to let go of my painful, fearful experiences.

I was outraged over the murder of millions, and in turn, I felt murderous and ready to kill. At that moment I was caught in the past, caught in finding fault, caught in separation. I'm sharing this experience with you so that you can see that even when we've worked with the attitudinal healing principles, we're not always willing to let go of our painful, fearful experiences. But we have to have compassion for ourselves anyway. In that moment, what I most needed was compassion for my state of mind. Compassion came to me in the form of the tour guide, who quickly grabbed the two men and ushered them out of the castle.

I stood there totally embarrassed because I had lost it. I had been a madwoman, ready to kill. I felt such vulnerability at knowing that I was capable of murder. I had let these two men upset me to that degree. As I think back on the experience, I reflect on a number of attitudinal healing principles: We can let go of the past and of the future. We can learn to love ourselves and others by forgiving rather than judging. And, finally: Because love is eternal, death need not be viewed as fearful. I realized that if it's really true that there is no death, then we can't really kill our enemies, and we can't really kill anyone to get rid of them. We are called upon to forgive and heal, and no matter how old an atrocity is, at some point there must be forgiveness, the healing balm of our pain.

I think again of President Clinton's words about racism being a curse on America. For our country to heal, we have to open up these wounds and say, "I'm sorry. We made a mistake. It was wrong." I think we're beginning to do that now because our hearts are finally big enough to do it.

Back there at the Elmina Castle, the tour guide returned, and when he came up to me, I said to him, "Sir, I really want to apologize for my behavior. I really behaved badly. I could have done this differently. I'm very sorry for my behavior, and I really want you to know that I would not really have done anything to hurt them. I want to ask your forgiveness for my behavior, and I really want those two men to know that I'm sorry that I behaved that way." I knew I had behaved in an ugly way, and I recalled the abuses I had heaped upon them as they were hurrying away.

As I apologized to the tour guide, I was choosing again. We can always choose and direct ourselves to be peaceful inside regardless of what is happening outside, but sometimes we make other choices. And in those times we must learn to show compassion for ourselves and ask for forgiveness.

Now I know those Dutch fellows saw the murder in my eyes, and they had left very quickly when the tour guide escorted them away from the scene. I think at that point they had realized that racism is truly a life-threatening illness. But we don't have to get stuck with this cyclic pain that keeps us wounded and then inflicts wounds and continues on a day-to-day basis. We can do the heart work to break the cycle.

For me the process continued when I got back home to California. We went to visit Jerry Jampolsky to take him a gift from Africa and share with him our journey. Jerry knew about the work we were doing to build a center for children in Ghana, and he said to me, "Aeeshah, I have a friend who's from Holland, and he's looking to make a donation to some worthy work. Do you have a project you might be interested in sharing with him that needs some funding?"

As soon as I heard the word "Holland," I thought that since I was in the process of healing my attitude toward Dutch people, I didn't feel quite ready to meet Jerry's friend.

It would take four years before full reconciliation and completion would come to this situation. Jerry's Dutch friend came to California in 1996. He was also a friend of Matthew Fox, the writer and theologian, who had recently opened the University of Creation Spirituality in downtown Oakland. One morning, our telephone rang, and it was Jerry's Dutch friend saying he would be in Oakland at 9:00 A.M. to visit Matthew Fox, and he wondered if he could stop by to visit our Attitudinal Healing Center in Oakland. We were excited at the prospect of meeting our new friend from Holland. We couldn't pass up the opportunity, and it so happens that Jerry's Dutch friend is now my friend, and I've healed my experience with Dutch people.

Retrieving Our Past

When members of the Akan Tribe of West Africa speak of the Sankofa bird, the bird that retrieves its past as it moves forward, they offer us a wonderful image for healing. In a sense, we are all called upon to do what the Sankofa bird does, if we truly desire to live our lives in the present moment. We must all look at ways to retrieve ourselves when we start to fall under the spell of the past. To retrieve ourselves, we need only look at our past through the eyes of spirit, through the eyes of wholeness. In this way we can glean from it what we truly want from life right now.

When President Clinton and others first suggested a national apology for racism and for slavery, many people got upset and demanded to know why we would want to open up the past. They missed the point altogether! The only spiritually valid reason to explore the past is to bring healing in the present.

The beautiful thing about being human is that we can always correct our errors. We can look at our errors and our mistakes, we can acknowledge them as errors, and we can move on.

We have explored a bit about letting go of the past. Given that we all want to achieve future goals in our lives, how do we also let go of the future? What does letting go of the future mean? Is it possible to live in the moment? Learning the art of dialogue can be a helpful process to internalize this option. To let go of the past and the future is to allow forgiveness to erase all memory of our painful emotional upsets in the past as well as our concerns and expectations of the future. Only then can we live in the present and experience our true reality, which is love. As we practice this principle, we realize the truth of the first principle, "The essence of our being is love." When we let go of the past, whether it is negative or positive, we leave ourselves to experience the present, which in turn allows us to release expectations of the future.

PUTTING PRINCIPLE #4 INTO PRACTICE

"We can let go of the past and of the future."

1. Our collective historical race relations have been long and painful. Can we live our day-to-day life without attachments to the past? You witnessed my inability to let go of the past. I was absolutely ready to do bodily injury to the two men from Holland out at Elmina Castle over a 500-year-old atrocity. Attitudinal healing principle #4 helped me alleviate the shame I experienced after getting so angry that day at the castle. I was able to take a few moments to acknowledge my feelings. Feelings that are denied cannot be released; feelings imprison us until they are acknowledged. I also acknowledged that

the abuse is not happening now, which also helped me let go of the feelings of hurt and rage. Finally, I explored what I could have done differently. I found that dialogue in a safe environment was helpful. When you face a similar situation, remember:

- Acknowledge your feelings triggered by the past.
- Recognize that the past event is not taking place now, and let go of the feelings it has triggered. Forgive yourself for your unconscious reactions.
- Explore what you could have done differently, perhaps by dialoguing with a trusted friend.

2. Most of us go through life believing yesterday's hurt must inevitably become today's pain and tomorrow's torment. We carry our past experiences in the form of negative and positive emotions. Our negative emotions based in race prejudices can be described as fears we have had in the past and continue to relive in the present. We can be greatly assisted in letting go of the past by taking time every day to explore the feelings that come up for us when we are experiencing a situation that is painful. Consider these steps:

- Ask yourself: Am I totally in the present with the situation, or am I reliving a past hurt that may trigger additional emotional upsets?
- Take a five minute time-out. Stop thinking and start breathing.
- Slowly repeat the principle, allowing yourself to feel the words: "I can let go of the past and of the future."

3. When you become aware that a circumstance in the present is triggering a charged racial memory from the past, take the following steps:

- Take a sheet of paper, perhaps in your journal. Settle down in a comfortable spot and take three long, deep breaths.

- Write about what is coming up for you. What memories are surfacing? What messages from the past have you internalized about race? Spend an additional three minutes jotting down your thoughts, feelings, and associations.

- Let yourself know that you have a choice. You can now choose to let go of the past, let go of the future, and open yourself up to experiencing the present as it truly is.

CHAPTER EIGHT

Each Precious Instant

A vertical line is dignity.
The horizontal line is peaceful.
The obtuse line is action.
That's universal, it is primary.

JANET COLLINS

ATTITUDINAL HEALING PRINCIPLE #5

"Now is the only time there is, and each instant is for giving."

Many current systems of philosophy speak of the importance of the present moment. The fifth principle of attitudinal healing emphasizes the value of forgiveness in letting go of the past. We will not be able to be in the present without forgiveness. True forgiveness acts as an erasure and eliminates all past hurts. This principle is very powerful because it acknowledges our ability to heal all past mistakes in the moment. No matter how long we are plagued with the pain that racism brings, we can always let it go in the present. This principle allows us to embrace all that we are in the instant.

When we let go of our fear about racism, we can explore our ability to make corrections in the present. In truth, there is no other time. All our injustices can continue right now, or all our injustices can end right now. Are we willing to forgive each instant?

Gerd's Story

One of the most powerful examples of the fifth principle of attitudinal healing, "Now is the only time there is, and each instant is for giving," was demonstrated by a new friend, Gerd. Gerd was born in Germany before World War II. He came to one of our Healing Racism Workshops and touched everyone deeply with his story. Gerd came with a strong interest in healing racism and was actively working on healing his attitude and forgiving himself. He realized the truth of the fifth principle when he woke up one day and remembered that thirty-three years ago he had fathered a mixed race daughter he had turned his back on.

He described himself in this way: "I am the war child of a retired Nazi storm trooper, and it recently came to my attention that I left my daughter in Liberia in 1963 two months before she was born. Now, all I have of her are two pictures and three strings of beads—a very personal souvenir of her mother, and a whole new way of hearing the country song 'I'm in love with you, baby, and I don't even know your name.'"

As Gerd shared his story, he had the attention of the entire group. We were a mixture of whites, Jews, African Americans, Chinese, and Hispanics. Everyone was open and receptive to Gerd's process. Gerd was very clear that he had come a long way from the racial arrogance, self-righteousness, "cultural colonialism," and hatred he was born into. He had lived in a war zone in Germany as a child during World War II, and his father was a Nazi storm trooper. He told of being six years old and listening from a bomb shelter to the British bombing the city. He grew up and left Germany in the late 1950s and early 1960s to work as an engineer in Africa.

Gerd talked vividly of his stay in Liberia. He had moved past his shame into a place of healing. He openly described how

109

he had come to live in Liberia and shared with us slides he had taken thirty-five years before. He had a job with the Dodge Company to go to Liberia and extract oil and all kinds of minerals from the mountains. We were shocked to see that this corporation had literally mowed a whole mountain down. It was quite amazing to see that there was no regard or respect for the environment and no respect for the people. Gerd's work involved moving a mountain of ore. He showed us slides of roads and railroads being built by the combined efforts of Great Britain, Germany, and the United States to move precious ore from Liberia to Europe and America, to improve the lives of the people who live in these areas. He spoke of remembering the "lush green rain forest of Mount Nimba being dotted by the ironwood trees turning red as the dry season progressed." However, as we watched the progression of the slide show, we observed that by the time the engineers had completed their job a whole mountain of minerals had been moved from Liberia.

Africa has fed the world with its rich minerals and served the world with its vast source of human slave labor. The West could not be a world power without the raw materials taken from Africa, many times free of charge. Today Africa is still not included as a part of the world in a healthy and respectful way. Only recently we (Kokomon and Aeeshah) were refused a life insurance policy because we had traveled to West Africa. It is on the list of dangerous countries to travel to, and is considered a threat to world health.

Gerd explained to us that had he had more love and respect for the culture he was living in, he would not have ended up as he is today. His personal dilemma is shared by many like him, white and black. He is now looking for his daughter, whom he has never seen. However, he was able to put together a computer picture of what she should look like at thirty-four years of age.

At the workshop Gerd told us, "This is my personal challenge, and I will respond to it from the deepest level of my intuitive heart. And it is exactly that space that tells me that my personal story is also a holographic miniature of the white man's participation in the pain of a whole continent." Gerd's story helped us all see the value of forgiveness in our lives and the value of the timelessness of all things. One day, Gerd was a single man with no children; then, through a spiritual awakening, he woke up to the truth that he is a father of a lovely mixed-race daughter in Liberia and could possibly be a grandfather, too. He spoke of learning more about love and forgiveness in the last few months than in the previous fifty-eight years of his life.

Gerd is now actively involved in human rights work in Liberia, because he is intimately aware that Africa is part of the whole and that what happens in Africa affects him personally. He is aware of his responsibility to stop the violence wherever it is occurring. He knows personally that every human being is someone else's daughter or son and deserves the same love, attention, and respect that he now feels for his own daughter.

Tom's Story

Tom Pinkson holds a Ph.D. in psychology. He works as a clinical consultant at the Center for Attitudinal Healing in Sausalito, California. We know him as Tomas, our urban shaman, and hold him close to our heart. He has supported the healing racism work that we do by being an active participant in our Healing Racism Circles. Walking in two worlds, the shamanic world of indigenous spirituality and the Western world as a practicing psychologist, he is the founder and president of the Wakan, a nonprofit, spiritually based educational community. He is an author, teacher, and public speaker.

In this section, Tomas shares in his own words his journey to reconnect with an old friend whom he knew only as a powerful connection that totally embraced the essence of our being, which is love. Tomas shares powerfully how he reached back into time and was able to experience the truth "Now is the only time there is, and each instant is for giving."

While in the Washington, D.C., area visiting my dad, who was struggling with cancer, I (Tomas) decided to track down an old junior high friend of mine I had not seen since shortly after our graduation from high school. We met in seventh grade through sports and grew to be close friends. Our usual routine after sports practice at school was to walk several miles home together, before he would split off to his neighborhood and me to mine, talking about anything and everything that came to our minds. It was a deep connection, and while we didn't have a language or consciousness with which to express it, I think we both felt a real sense of brotherhood, a soul connection. And yet, as so often happens in life, when I moved out to California after high school we lost touch.

But seeing my dad and being touched by the fragility of life, something inside me said remember those of your past that you felt the strong connection with and would like to see again. Butch immediately came to mind. I tried calling Information, but there was no listing. On the way back from picking up some Chinese food to go, I went past his old neighborhood and decided, what the hell, I might as well give it a try. So I drove down the narrow street of what used to be "the other side of the tracks," where the black people lived, and found an old timer sitting out in his yard enjoying the afternoon sun.

I stopped the car, got out, and walked over to him. "I've got a strange request," I said. "I'm trying to find an old friend of mine who lived around here in the 1950s. You know a guy named Butch?" His face lit up. Butch had been well known in the old neighborhood. He was a leader even then, well respected even by the men in the "hood." The old man turned and pointed. "Yeah sure, I know Butch. He lives right around the corner." My heart jumped in excitement. I drove around the corner and in the middle of the block a group of men were playing with kids. I asked if they knew where Butch lived, and they signaled the house I was in front of. "Do you know if he's home?" I asked. "Yeah, he's home. He just finished cutting the grass. He's around back." Now I was really excited.

I knocked at the front door, and a big bruiser answered. He identified himself as Butch's son, and I told him I was an old friend of his father and was there to surprise him and "blow his mind." The son immediately got the spirit of my surprise and played along. I walked out around the house to the backyard, where Butch was relaxing on the porch with his wife and daughter. Being a trickster by heart, I figured I would mess with him a bit—after all, what a great setup I had!

I went roaring up onto his porch yelling, "Butch, I'm going to kick your ass!" He jumped up, not knowing what to expect. I charged right up into his face. "You don't know who I am do you?" I said in a softer voice. "No, I sure don't," he replied with a perplexed frown on his forehead. Then I told him who I was, and a big grin came over his face. We collapsed into a big hug. His mind was definitely blown. Afterward he introduced me to his family, and we sat down and had a wonderful visit. He was very touched by my seeking him out after all these years, and I shed a few tears as I talked about how I felt a soul connection from long ago and I didn't want to see that lost if we had a chance to reconnect. "You were a for-real friend, Tom," he said in his southern Maryland accent.

We talked about the time I had invited him to join me one Saturday morning at my neighborhood's local pool to go swimming. Butch had said he would like to go, but then two separate times that we set up a time to meet, he never showed. That wasn't like him, and I didn't understand what was going on. Butch was strangely quiet when I confronted him about it. Later, when talking about the incident with one of the other guys in the neighborhood who knew Butch from the sports teams we played on together, I found out what was going on. "He didn't come to the pool," explained the older guy, "because he knew he wouldn't be able to come in." I was stunned. In my naiveté and unconsciousness of youth, I had no idea that this was what it was all about. But Butch knew. He lived in that reality of the South, and where we lived in Maryland was below the Mason-Dixon Line; it *was* the South! Now we were able to talk about it, as men. And the heart-line to friendship deepened even more.

We went on to talk about all the old guys we grew up with, some real characters, and how they were doing today. Most of them were doing pretty well, I was happy to hear. I was particularly interested to hear about one friend of ours, a white guy from a working class background who was just a real good human being. He was a big guy, a great athlete, with no attitude and a kind heart to go along with it. He was another good brother from a time when boys didn't have an okay to talk about feelings for each other.

114

"Doug, oh yeah, he still lives around here," Butch told me. "Stopped by a while ago and we still see each other now and then. You know, Doug was like you, a real friend. I remember once in high school at a track meet where I was running the high hurdles. I was really moving and won the race. Just as I was getting to the finish line, I heard some cracker yell, 'Man, that nigger can really run.' It pissed me off, and as soon as I passed the finish line I went back to confront the guy because I saw who did it. But the coach stopped me. He said Doug had already taken care of it. 'What did he do?' I asked. Coach said Doug went over to the guy and got right in his face. Coach heard Doug tell him, 'You say that word again, and I'll be the nigger you're dealing with!'

"Like I said," Butch went on, "Doug was a big guy, and when he was angry not too many people would argue with him. He made me proud to be a man, standing up for what's right, protecting dignity, affirming justice—a real caretaker. He demonstrated what I believe to be one of our chief responsibilities: to care for life, to nourish it, to protect it, to honor it. This takes courage and it takes love. My old friend Doug did it then. I pray that I and my other brothers can do it today," Butch concluded.

PUTTING PRINCIPLE #5 INTO PRACTICE

"Now is the only time there is, and each instant is for giving."

1. You can put the principle "Now is the only time there is, and each instant is for giving" into practice to expedite your healing by affirming the following:

- I will take time each day to be still and listen to my inner spirit while I recall any intolerant attitudes and heal them.

- I will take time to commune with nature and to forgive my parents if they taught me hatred of people of other races, cultures, or creeds.

- I will accept and acknowledge people who look different from me.

2. If you feel any resistance to accepting differences, repeat to yourself, slowly: There is beauty in diversity. There is beauty in diversity. There is beauty in diversity.

3. Remind yourself each day that now is the only time there is, thereby reinforcing a new attitude. Then say to yourself:

- In this instant I release any attitude that I may have that is grounded in race prejudices. Discriminating against anyone because of race, creed, or color robs me of my true gifts.

- As I experience peace and love this day, I am awakening to the profound truth that I cannot have peace and love unless I want the same for everyone I encounter.

CHAPTER NINE

Forgiving Rather Than Judging

The supreme personality of Godhead said:
Compassion toward every living entity, forgiveness, and
freedom from both envy and the passion for honor—
these are the transcendental qualities.

THE BHAGAVAD GITA

ATTITUDINAL HEALING PRINCIPLE #6

"We can learn to love ourselves and others by forgiving rather than judging."

Let's face it! Healing racism can feel like an almost insurmountable task to undertake. We are not sharing our stories with the primary goal of changing society. Our goal in sharing our story is to continue the process of solidity in our own healing process. In sharing our hearts with you, our readers, we hope that perhaps you will decide to join us on the road to healing. We know that our own process is enhanced by your joining us on the road to wholeness, and we thank you for the support. We hope that one day we all find ourselves in the place where we are learning solely in joy, love, and peace.

We know that the very idea that we have to learn to love ourselves and others puts us in a place of needing to do inner work on ourselves. Self-love is the focus of this chapter. To come into the understanding that we are beautiful, intelligent, and abundant in all areas of our life means learning to value our spiritual beauty. Only through this awareness will we be able to give up judgment as a tool to define our essence. The understanding that "the essence of our being is love" opens the doors to the truth of what forgiveness can do to heal the wounds of racism, as we let the past go. Forgiveness opens the doors of creativity, and true reconciliation becomes possible. Judgment, on the other hand, opens the wounds of racism and increases our level of hopelessness and fear that racism and its effects will never end.

The Need for Atonement

Forgiveness is probably the most powerful healing agent in the universe, and it arises directly out of the awareness that the essence of our being is love. When wrong has been done, forgiveness is needed to allow the healing of both the wrong-doer and the wronged. Our nation remains mired in the suspicion and mistrust engendered by centuries of racist policy and practice. We have not done the work of forgiveness, and so we cannot move on to a new America free forever from the blight of racism.

But forgiveness flowers best when there has been genuine atonement. As President Clinton said at a speech at U.C. San Diego, "We have torn down the barriers in our lives; now we must break down the barriers in our minds and our hearts. That is the unfinished work of our time—to lift the burden of race and redeem the promise of America." Indeed, this is the true heart work of our time, and how do we go about accomplishing it?

Sometimes when I (Kokomon) reflect upon this, I am struck by how much I have suffered in this country simply because I was born in Africa and have black skin. I pay taxes just like everyone else. I work very hard and am a law-abiding citizen. When I see people rushing for an elevator, I hold the door open. Yet I have been mistreated as a worker solely on the basis of my race. I have been treated with suspicion and fear solely because of the color of my skin. It is a true dilemma.

There is an African proverb that says: "If you offend, ask for pardon; if offended, forgive." In America, we need to put into practice both aspects of this wisdom. The first step is to acknowledge that something wrong has happened. As another African proverb says: "The one who consumes his [or her] disease cannot expect to be cured." Yes, when we consume our disease and bury it deep within us, it can never be cured. We must bring the disease up into the light of day, out in the open where we can have honest dialogue about it. This is what we must do with the disease of racism.

We can begin by acknowledging our pain, and then engaging in an open dialogue. Some talk about compensation. We aren't even ready for that discussion. First, we simply have to acknowledge the need for a dialogue. Another African proverb states: "Talking with one another is loving another." This is the foundation for forgiving one another.

Forget about compensation; forget about money or other possible demands. Is there really any way to pay with dollars for the suffering of hundreds of years of slavery and brutal discrimination? Talking with one another is the first step toward atonement, the first step towards forgiveness.

Politics aside, President Clinton took a tremendous stride forward just by bringing up the subject of racism as a topic for serious discussion. This is how we begin. And a true leader works to bring people together. If years from now people can look back and say that we truly began an honest dialogue, then we will have given a most precious gift to America, and indeed to the whole world. As Marianne Williamson writes in *The Healing of America*, "In order to heal, America must atone for our violations against others, without which no true reconciliation among ourselves, or with other nations, is possible. We cannot move forward until we have made a serious effort to clean up the past." Williamson stresses the importance of a national apology and atonement as steps in the right direction. Using the principles of attitudinal healing, we can all be part of this important initiative.

Young People Show the Way

On occasion we have had the opportunity to present our Healing Racism program to young people. Recently, we were invited to present our workshop to an organization called YES, which is an acronym for Youth for Environmental Sanity. They organize youth camps for young people to come and learn about the environment and what young people can do to impact the environmental movement. This particular camp was focused on the world's youth leaders. Forty of the world's most powerful leaders in the youth environmental movement from twenty-four nations converged in Santa Cruz, California, for a weeklong gathering to build, network, and develop skills. This group wanted to include in their training the devastating effect of environmental racism.

We had connected with this group through Ocean Robbins at John Denver's Windstar Symposium in 1995. Ocean felt strongly that his organization could benefit from the work that we were doing on racism. Therefore, he referred us to his father and mother, John and Deo Robbins. We knew about John Robbins through his book *Diet for a New America*, a best-selling book on the dietary link to environment and health. John called us wanting to know when our next Healing Racism Workshop would be. We gave him the date, and he and Deo signed up immediately.

John was impressed with our workshop and told us that he had been helped personally in the process. He and Deo demonstrated their connection with this work by attending three of our full-day sessions and by encouraging their staff at EarthSave to take the workshop as well. EarthSave is an international, nonprofit organization founded by John. It is dedicated to healthy people and a healthy planet. John realized that without racial healing his dream of a healthy people and a healthy planet would be futile.

We were honored and excited to have the opportunity to share with the young people at the YES Camp. We know that they will face great challenges as they move forward into the next millennium. They are going to be our future leaders, so all the unresolved issues from our generation are going to fall on their shoulders.

The young people at the YES camp were troubled about the emotional and the environmental state of our planet, our home. They were concerned about the serious social issues affecting the environmental issues of the day. They were asking important questions about how to come to a common ground of one family, respecting, loving, and understanding one another. We felt privileged to be there because we were learning so much from these young people.

As the camp went on, the young people focused on how we as Homo sapiens could "learn to love ourselves and others by forgiving rather than judging." They felt that they would be at a loss for solutions unless they learned to forgive those who came before them. They had expressed many judgments toward their elders, because they felt they were handed the baggage of pain, guilt, shame, and frustration from the years of prejudice and hatred of their ancestors. One young person expressed that she could not talk about race with her parents, because her parents did not have the tools to talk about racism.

The issue of forgiveness came up, including President Clinton's suggestion to set up a commission to start a dialogue on racism and possibly ask for forgiveness or perhaps send an apology to African Americans and also to Native Americans. One young woman said, "I don't think an apology is going to work. What good will it do, and how effective will an apology be? And besides, I was not living when all these horrible things happened. Why should I have to apologize for something I did not do? I have not offended anyone." Another young man said, "We may not have been there, but we are benefactors of the privileges that came with the problems." Another young woman said, "I think it would be a waste of time and energy. But I do think that after learning about all the madness that has occurred in the past, perhaps we could set aside a day—a day which would be a holiday that would honor all of our ancestors, a day of forgiveness and reconciliation."

We were profoundly moved by the work that these young people were doing on this issue. They expressed their gratitude for us creating this space for them to look more deeply into this issue. Many of them said that many times adults do not realize the pain that young people go through because they have not been given tools to deal with the issue of racism. Most times adults assume that young people do not have to deal with these issues because they feel that we now live in a "color-blind society." One young woman said she felt the pain of racism every day from her black counterparts at school. She said she has not been able to make a black friend and feels rejected by them daily at school. She also explained that going home to share this with her parents would not alleviate her situation, because they would wonder why she wanted a black friend.

Many of these young people come from affluent homes in the United States and from around the world. They feel deeply about environmental issues and wonder if there will be a world for them to live in. Our hearts were deeply touched by these young people, and we left the YES Camp recommitting ourselves to the sixth principle of attitudinal healing. One young man from Ghana, West Africa, declared, "I feel strongly that love is an answer to the problems of humanity and I want to be part of a global network that will utilize love as a ground of being to build a brighter future for all." We ended the session thanking these young people for their strength, courage, and vision for a better world. We shared with them a quote from Bishop Tutu that has been a source of strength and guidance for us:

Apartheid was and is immoral, evil, sinful, and blasphemous. We cannot ignore that. The consequences of apartheid cannot be wiped away simply by democratic decision-making structures, or even by the allocation of large sums of money for housing, education, health, and job creation.

When spouses in a marriage have quarreled, they cannot restore their relationship until one of the parties says those three most difficult words in any language: "I am sorry." If they try to skate over the difficulties, if they try to paper over the cracks, there is no healing.

The problem will fester and one day explode in a way that is devastation for both of them. Social relationships are

*the same: We cannot rebuild South Africa successfully
unless we address the emotional and spiritual factors
which have profoundly affected people's motivation.*

*Confession will be balm for the wounds in the hearts
of the victims of apartheid, but is also important
for the well-being of the perpetrators and for
their rehabilitation as human beings.*

*Guilt, even unacknowledged guilt, has a negative effect
on the guilty. Whether they know it or not, if they do not
confess they will be weighed down by this burden.*

DESMOND TUTU

We left the YES workshop knowing that tomorrow's ancestors indeed are formulating and planting the seeds of healing that will lead to the oneness that we all are longing for today.

Forgiving Rather Than Judging

*There is no need to learn through pain. And gentle lessons
are acquired joyously, and remembered gladly. What gives
you happiness you want to learn and not forget. It is not this
you would deny. Your question is whether the means by
which this course is learned will bring to you the joy it
promises. If you believed it would, the learning of it would be
no problem. You are not a happy learner yet because you still
remain uncertain that vision gives you more than judgment
does, and you have learned that both you cannot have.*

A COURSE IN MIRACLES

Forgiveness means letting go of the past and is therefore the means for correcting and healing the painful feelings that we hold from the past. These misperceptions can only be undone through the arduous process of letting go whatever we think other people may have done to us or whatever we may think we did to them. Through forgiveness, we can stop the endless recycling of guilt and look upon ourselves and others with love. Forgiveness allows us to let go of all that separates us from one another. Without the belief in separation, we can accept our own healing and send healing love to all those around us. Healing then becomes the torch of unity. As we recognize and claim inner peace, forgiveness becomes our single goal and our single function. When we accept both our function and our goal, we find that listening to our inner intuitive voice as the source for direction becomes our only guide to fulfillment. We are released as we release others from the prison of our distorted and illusory perceptions and join with them in the unity of love.

Whenever I (Kokomon) notice myself starting to feel a sense of separation, or whenever I start focusing on what other people have done to me or what I've done to them, I take this as a reminder. So as I recall some past painful incident, time and time again I remember to ask myself: Do I really want to be happy? Do I really want to have peace? And I recognize that my choice is this: Do I want to be happy and at peace or do I want to be caught in the pain of conflict and fear? Jerry Jampolsky taught me that whenever I see someone as guilty, I am reinforcing my own feelings of guilt and unworthiness. I cannot forgive myself unless I am willing to forgive others. And I cannot find peace and happiness within if I have not forgiven myself.

It does not matter what I think anyone has done to me in the past or what I think I may have done. Only through forgiveness can my release from guilt and fear be complete. And so today I choose to let go of all my past misperceptions about myself and others. Instead I will join with everyone and say that I see everyone only in the light of true forgiveness. I have made the commitment to heal myself, in accordance with the old adage: Healer, heal thyself. Before I can go out and share my journey of healing, so others may benefit and emulate this modeling and heal themselves, I must first heal myself. Mahatma Gandhi once said, "Confession of error is like a broom that sweeps away dirt and leaves the surface cleaner than before." He further stated: "To err is human. By confession, we convert our mistakes into stepping-stones for advance."

As I travel along my path, I have found it very important to apologize immediately for any error of any kind, and to be sincere about it, because there is no escape from it. It will follow you around forever if you let it. Gandhi also said, "There can never be Truth where there is no courage. There is no defeat in the confession of one's error; the confession itself is a victory." So when we find the courage to overcome our shame and confess our errors, we acknowledge the law of compensation, known in India as the law of karma, or cause and effect, and we immediately put to rest the consequences of errors rather than letting them compound over time with the added complication of deception and cover-up.

This principle can best be learned through the power of listening and the power of silence. If we are not able to listen, we will never be aware of our judgments about race and how forgiveness can release us from all past and present condemnations.

The roots of racism and nonacceptance of people who are different lie in fear. The seeds were planted long before any of us were born. Somehow along the way, we perceived ourselves as unloved and unlovable and projected this lack of love onto others.

If practiced sincerely, the sixth principle of attitudinal healing takes us beyond intolerance and racism, because it encourages us to love ourselves first. Then we can reinforce this love by extending it to others.

PUTTING PRINCIPLE #6 INTO PRACTICE

"We can learn to love ourselves and others by forgiving rather than judging."

1. This principle is easier said than done, but we have found that when we put it into practice, it frees the spirit to be in a state of peace. To deepen your experience of this principle, it might be helpful to practice a few listening skills.

2. Forgiveness acts as a soothing balm to release hardened matter stored in our memory banks that keeps the pain of the past as an active block to a peaceful state of mind. Set aside approximately thirty minutes for the following experience.

Be Still and Listen

- This exercise is about letting go and learning to love yourself and others through forgiveness.
- Listen. . . . Listen. . . . Listen. . . .
- Now allow yourself to remember prejudicial racial feelings, thoughts, or experiences about yourself or others that you are still holding on to.

- Just listen. . . . Allow yourself to have these feelings, to remember these thoughts, experience the past. . . . Do nothing. . . . Just listen. . . .

- As you listen and recall these experiences, ask yourself: What benefit do I receive from holding onto these negative feelings? How is the past serving me now? Am I able to forgive? How do I experience racism? How do I contribute to this dilemma?

- Continue to listen for at least ten more minutes.

- Now say to yourself quietly and gently: I can let all negative racial feelings go simply by choosing to forgive.

- Say to yourself: I understand that this instant I can undo all my prejudicial attitudes about race and the "other" simply by letting go. I can stop the cycle of blame through forgiveness. Forgiveness is recognizing that love can heal all pain. Forgiveness is choosing to look at our mistakes, and deciding to correct them with love. Forgiveness is being willing to say "I am sorry."

CHAPTER TEN

Becoming Love Finders

Alone, all alone
Nobody, but nobody
Can make it out here alone.

MAYA ANGELOU

ATTITUDINAL HEALING PRINCIPLE #7

"We can become love finders rather than fault finders."

We have been so conditioned to paying attention to skin tone that most times we are not aware of how strongly our attractions and repulsions are related directly to how we respond to color. If you were to enter a room filled with a race of people who were different from you, what would your experience be?

Because of our social conditioning, when we first meet someone racially different, we usually start by looking for faults. This principle of attitudinal healing states that instead we can become love finders. The key word is *can;* we don't have to—it is a choice. Our own personal experience of racial healing has shown us that when we become love finders, we feel better. Fault finding along racial lines usually serves as a means to lower the value of, or make ourselves feel better than, the "other." In this way, fault finding serves as a means to justify an illusory sense of superiority.

To become a love finder requires us to be vigilant and self-realized. Most of us are just regular, ordinary people; therefore, vigilance will be our primary tool for taking note of our blaming and fault finding. In order to be love finders, we must be willing to stop the fault finding so that the love finding can surface. To be love finders requires us to first love ourselves, which also means to be free of fear.

We have met some wonderful people through our Healing Racism Workshops, and we believe that their stories are significant for others who are struggling to look more deeply into racism and ways to bring healing to this elusive and sometimes volatile issue. Many of the people who attend our sessions on healing racism are baby boomers and were hopeful during the 1960s when the civil rights movement was at its peak. These same people became cynical when their heroes such as the Reverend Dr. Martin Luther King, Jr. and President Kennedy and other heroic people lost their lives trying to bring change in the racial arena.

Many of us expressed a great deal of despair because we were learning the hard way that the way people think cannot be legislated. It was difficult for us to accept that we had legally integrated our society but that emotionally we appeared more separated than ever along racial lines. The Healing Racism Circles as well as the workshops became a place to begin a dialogue to look more deeply into our emotional blocks to accepting and loving one another unconditionally.

Many of the people who have attended our sessions have became friends and supporters of the work that we do. Many times we have been told by participants how much they admire our courage to tackle such a difficult problem. We always commend them for joining us on this journey to racial healing, because we knew at a heart level we could never do this work alone.

Other people's stories are powerful, too, and hearing their stories has helped us to continue the work that we do. There are many reasons why they choose to come to a Healing Racism Workshop or Circle. The most important thing for us is that they have come. We believe that it only takes a little willingness to start the process of learning to see differently, learning to become love finders. It is that little willingness that made the difference between a choice for peace and joining or a choice for conflict and separation.

Ron's Story

One remarkable man has been coming to our Healing Racism Circles for about a year now; however, we have known him for about ten years. We first met him at the Center for Attitudinal Healing in Tiburon. Ron Alexander was forty-three years old then. He is fifty-three now and feels more grounded in the principles of attitudinal healing. When we first met him, Ron's thick southern accent gave him away immediately. He had grown up in South Carolina. When we first knew Ron, he never talked openly about his life in the South or what it was like for him growing up in an apartheid situation. It was only recently that we learned of his deep interest in racial healing. Ron is a counselor by profession and a wonderful human being.

At one of our dialogues Ron spoke openly about his upbringing and his struggle to come to terms with it. He spoke about being taught as a child that "black people had their place and as long as they kept their place they were okay." He said, "I was taught that they were unclean and inferior. I was so racist, I could not listen to Dr. Martin Luther King, Jr. because of his accent." It was amazing to hear Ron's comment on Dr. King's accent, because Ron spoke with the same southern accent that Dr. King spoke with.

Ron's journey to healing began when he began to grow spiritually and educate himself through traveling overseas.

This opened his mind to the variety of groups of people speaking different languages, and he realized that all he spoke was English. He told of reading the life of Krishnamurti. It was then that he began to reach out to people of color. Ron spoke of his healing truly beginning when he was able to look at differences and learn to be a love finder rather than a fault finder. He said when he was in the South, listening to Dr. Martin Luther King, Jr. was difficult: "He was too black. I was too prejudiced. I could not hear what he was saying." In the last few years Ron has changed his life by changing his heart about racial differences, and he has also read Dr. King's speeches and many books about the civil rights movement. He has come to realize what a brilliant man Dr. King was.

Ron Alexander has taken his change of heart and put it into action. Ron committed himself to working with other white men and women who he feels need to look more deeply into the concept of white privilege. Utilizing the principle "We can learn to be love finders rather than fault finders," Ron facilitates dialogues focused on internalizing racial healing. He recently moderated an interethnic panel discussion on nonviolence. He also was very active in launching the Season of Nonviolence, which commemorates the assassination of Mahatma Gandhi on January 30 in 1948 and Martin Luther King, Jr.'s assassination in 1968. Ron Alexander's transformation validates what can happen when there is a true willingness to see differently.

PUTTING PRINCIPLE #7 INTO PRACTICE

"We can become love finders rather than fault finders."

132

1. Read these reminders slowly and repeat every two or three days over the next six weeks:

- I understand that by becoming a love finder, I will recognize and honor all beings with affection and an open heart, no matter what their race, ethnic origin, religion, or creed. I am open to receive this same capacity of recognition, honor, and affection from all beings.

- I understand that all the faults I find in different races are actually my own faults reflecting back to me. It is as if I am looking in a mirror.

- This moment I release all my faulty assumptions and misinformation about other races.

- I commit this day to be a love finder from morning to night.

- I will be sensitive to fault finding grounded in racism that is made by my family, friends, or co-workers. I will find the courage to speak up.

2. Write down two choices you made today that stopped you from becoming a love finder. State two actions you can take that will move you toward being a love finder.

3. List five negative stereotypes you wish to eliminate that will help you to love more authentically across racial and cultural lines.

4. Be sure to acknowledge your progress along the way.

CHAPTER ELEVEN

Choices for Peace

The handbook of the strategist has said:
Do not invite the fight; accept it instead.
Better a foot behind than an inch too far ahead.

LAO-TZU

ATTITUDINAL HEALING PRINCIPLE #8

"We can choose and direct ourselves to be peaceful inside regardless of what is happening outside."

The eighth attitudinal healing principle reminds us that life is about choices. We may not be able to change the world, society, our community, our neighbor, or our family, but we can choose how we will respond to the world and to the people in our world.

As we have mentioned earlier, taking corrective action, such as speaking up in response to a racist statement or filing a legal suit in response to discrimination in a work setting, is sometimes necessary and appropriate. To heal ourselves of prejudicial and biased beliefs, however, goes beyond corrective action in the world and requires a personal commitment to inner peace and a feeling of connection to all of humanity. We begin to bring to life a line from one of John Denver's songs, "That child in the ghetto is my child," and we can come to believe that the lives of indigenous people in the rain forest are intimately connected with our lives in the city, with all its modern conveniences. When we have this awareness, this will help frame all of our choices. The following story suggests the tremendous power unleashed when we act from our capacity to choose.

Diapers for Sabah

My daughter recently gave birth to her first baby, so I (Aeeshah) am now a new grandma. Soon after the birth, I had an experience that reminded me once again that some people in this society are minimized and not given the same services as others. It was another opportunity for me to practice the principles of attitudinal healing, and choose and choose again.

I was so excited when my daughter gave birth to a beautiful little girl. This baby was born very early in the morning, and my daughter named her Sabah, which means morning. I was there when she was delivering. My daughter breathed deeply through the whole process and birthed the most beautiful daughter with no medication in a totally natural birth. The midwives and I were so excited. I wanted to start a campaign focusing on making breast milk a part of the gross national product, because I felt that if breast milk were part of the GNP, then women would be given a whole different status. Breast milk is simply the most powerful thing that Mother Nature has made, but it is not yet fully acknowledged in our country.

I was so excited when I got home, thinking of the powerful feminine principle my daughter and new grandbaby embodied, and I wanted to share with my granddaughter the gift of a diaper service. I knew my daughter didn't want to use disposable diapers since they go into landfills, causing a tremendous environmental problem. I decided to call up the diaper service I had used over twenty-five years before, when I had just given birth to my daughter.

The next morning, I called up the diaper service, and they were still in business. With excitement in my voice, I told them that I wanted to order three months of diaper service. The woman on the other end of the line, whose name was Debra, was most enthusiastic at the idea of making a sale for not just one week but three months of diaper service. Everything was going quite smoothly.

But when she took my daughter's address, Debra said, "One moment." She was gone for a few minutes, and then she came back and said, "Oh, I looked at your daughter's address, and it's below 980."

"Below 980?" I replied. "What does that have to do with anything?"

"Well, we don't deliver below 980" was her answer. Now, 980 is one of the freeways that defines West Oakland, and my daughter lives in West Oakland.

"Well, I really don't understand why," I said. "I used this service over twenty-five years ago, and I really want the best for my little grandbaby."

Debra stammered out some more excuses about another service they didn't want to compete with.

"Why don't you let me speak to the manager," I said, "because that just doesn't make sense."

So I introduced myself to the manager, and we exchanged greetings. I told him I wanted their diaper service and said I understood from Debra that they don't deliver below 980, but I didn't understand why. He explained to me that this was because of the violence in the neighborhood and concern for the safety of the drivers.

"Well, that sounds like redlining to me," I said, and I told him I had a very good friend named Jerry Brown, the ex-governor of California who was now hosting a radio show, and I thought this would make a good radio talk show about redlining around diaper services. It happened that we had met Jerry Brown early in 1994, soon after he moved to Oakland. He was living in an old warehouse near Jack London Square known as the American Bag Building. He was building a live-work space in the same block on Harrison Street, which now houses his We the People organization. We had called and set up a time to visit. When we arrived at his warehouse and rang the bell, the former governor of California had humbly raised the window and handed the front door key down to us. We maneuvered our way upstairs, and we could see that Jerry Brown had already begun to work on important issues affecting the city of Oakland (he has since been elected mayor). He was surprisingly accessible. We told him about our work, and he was very open to it. Since that time, he has donated the use of his auditorium many times for our Healing Racism Workshops. So I believed he would be interested in reporting on his radio show if there was redlining going on in Oakland.

After I mentioned this, the manager of the diaper service said, "Well, I can't really say that we redline; we don't redline."

"Well, if you don't deliver to certain neighborhoods, that's redlining," I explained while he went "no, no, no." And I said, "Well, my daughter really wants this service, and I really want this service, and I think it's worth a conversation. I think we at least need to dialogue, and the public needs to know what's happening with this."

Finally, he said perhaps there would be something he could do. So I went on and talked in detail with him about the environment and the value of diaper services and how he should be more than happy to make sure that every mother has an opportunity to use their service and use diapers. "Well, I tell you what," he told me. "What we'll do is we'll give you the service, but we can only deliver to your address. So I'm going to put Debra back on the phone."

So Debra came back on the phone, and I told her I was concerned that every week I would have to make sure that the diapers got to my daughter's house, which is about twenty blocks from my house, and she would have to bring the dirty diapers to me. "We're not happy with that," I said, "but my grandbaby deserves this service, so we're going to try to fig-ure out a way to do it."

So Debra took my address and went to check on it, and came back on after about three minutes. By this time I'd been on the phone for about twenty minutes with these people, trying to arrange diaper service. When Debra got back on the line, she told me, "Oh, ma'am, we don't deliver west of 580."

"You don't deliver west of 580! I don't understand. This just doesn't make sense. You're telling me you have a service and you don't deliver below 980 or west of 580? You're blocking off all of West Oakland! I'm having a really big problem with that. It means there's a whole group of people that does not and cannot get your service." I told her that I'd gotten their service over twenty-five years ago, but I lived in Berkeley at the time, and now I lived in West Oakland within minutes of Berkeley and I couldn't get the service even though the neighborhood is safe. So I asked to speak to the manager again.

So she went to get the manager, but instead of Tim, Debra came back on the line and told me, "Okay, we'll give you the service, but we can only deliver the diapers at 3:00 in the morning."

I remarked in surprise at the odd time, but told her I would check with my husband. I guess anyone else would have said forget it at this time, but Kokomon agreed to deal with it. So I went back to the phone and I said, "Okay, we'll accept it."

And Debra just shockingly said, "You'll accept it?" I guess what they assumed is that by saying 3:00 A.M. I would get upset and angry and decline the offer. I wonder if those who haven't ever had such an experience can imagine the kind of energy some people have to expend just to get basic services. "So you really want the service?" Debra asked. "Are you sure?"

So I set up the order and paid for it via credit card. When I got off the phone I was thinking how some children are born minimized, with a certain set place defined for them—when you're born with certain skin colors, you have a place, and society wants you to stay in your place. And my grandbaby, fresh and new out of the womb, beautiful and innocent, was being refused diaper service. But I refused to accept that.

I knew I would have to talk more with the people at the diaper service, but I let it rest for that day. The following day my daughter was coming home with her baby, so I went over to her house to help her get things ready. "Well, Amanah," I told her. "I got the diaper service for you." "You did?" she said. "Yes!" I replied. "But there's a problem; the problem is they can only deliver the service to my house at 3:00 A.M."

"Mom, how could you accept that?"

"Well, Amanah, I wanted the service for you, and so now what we'll do is call them back and talk with them some more, and maybe we can reason with them."

So I got on the phone, and I asked specifically to speak with Debra. When she got on the line, I reintroduced myself and told her about the service we'd ordered and that the delivery time and location were very difficult for my daughter. "Debra,"

I said, "can you imagine what it would be like if you were a new mom? How would you feel if you had to take your dirty diapers to your mama's house, then pick up your clean diapers every week for three months? As a woman, how would you feel? As a new mother, how would you feel?"

And I could feel that our hearts were touching at this point, and I remembered that the deepest essence of attitudinal healing is heart work. I was choosing to remain calm and at peace, despite this disturbing circumstance, and I was keeping my heart open as I explained things to Debra. For change to occur takes heart work, and you have to be willing to go the extra mile. Some people might have told me to just forget it, but when you live in this country and you've dealt with racism your whole life, there's a certain tenacity, commitment, and willingness to go the extra mile. And that's what I knew I needed to do. I had to go the extra mile to get the service for my grandbaby. She deserved it; she deserved the best this country had to offer. So I kept talking to Debra, telling her my daughter deserved the service, that my grandbaby deserved it, while all the time my daughter was listening in the background.

Then Debra said, "Okay, I really understand, and what I'm going to do is try to talk to the driver and see if the driver would be willing to come to your daughter's house and bring the diapers there, because you have paid for them already, and your daughter really does deserve that."

And I said, "Thank you, Debra." Sabah's diapers would be delivered directly to her front door. I believe that because I appealed to her heart, Debra was able to let her defenses down and realize that they had a stupid rule and that rule was based on racism, and making sure that certain people stay in their place.

Can you imagine how many people are refused this service? West Oakland is a large community. And if I had let it go, my grandbaby would never have received clean, laundered diapers from a diaper service.

Choices

When we were in Africa recently, we noticed that many people still live without refrigerators. Their lives without refrigerators afford us the opportunity to live with refrigerators—and delay the increasing holes in the ozone layer. Can you imagine if everyone in China and Africa began to drive gasoline-powered cars? Mother Earth could not handle the strain. We shared with a group of people who attended one of our workshops the sobering fact that more electricity is used in New York's Times Square in one day than is used in the whole country of Ghana in one month. The people in countries like Ghana are, in essence, affording us our so-called modern lifestyle. We can begin to make different choices that would increase peace for all of us. We are all connected, and we need one another. Racism is a moral issue that stems from greed, insecurity, and fear of scarcity.

When we realize that we can choose and direct ourselves to be peaceful inside regardless of what is happening outside, we eliminate the fundamental cause of racism, for racism is always based on fear and a sense of lack. So how do we manage to stay peaceful despite outer circumstances? This can only be accomplished through coming to the recognition of how we got here, recognizing our common ground.

Stories the world over share common threads on creation mythology. This story, as told from biblical times, points to how we got here. For a version in a nutshell, read this account from theologian Matthew Fox: "About 15 billion years ago this universe began, smaller than a pinprick. And it's been growing ever since, so now 15 billion years later the universe may be one trillion galaxies large, each with billions of stars. And this means that we're all connected. We're connected to all the galaxies, all the planets, all the stars in the universe; we're made of the same stuff. But part of the amazement is that if, in the first 750,000 years, the universe, which was a fireball, had expanded one millionth of a millionth of a second slower or faster than it did, we wouldn't be here today. And if the overall temperature of the original fireball over 750,000 years ago had been one degree warmer or colder than it was, one degree, we wouldn't be here today. We lucked out!"

Today modern physics reminds us that everything is alive with photons, which are light waves. We all have photons in us—whether we are black or white, Asian or Native American, straight or gay, rich or poor. Our self-esteem depends on love, on recognition that every person we see and meet on the street, in the bus, in the elevator, has an essence that is love. Once we come to this recognition, then of course the next level is to honor all beings. And once we have this perspective, we can easily see that peace is a choice available to us in any situation, and does not depend on external circumstances.

When we are faced with the challenge of choice, there is ultimately only one direction to go—into the wisdom that has been passed on through our elders and our ancestors, the sacred spiritual principles that lie at the heart of all religions.

Shifting one's own perspective has the power to create miracles. What it all comes down to is that place of oneness, that place of understanding. As Martin Luther King, Jr. once said, "Injustice anywhere is a threat to justice everywhere." Once we understand that we are one indivisible whole, we can remain peaceful even in the face of discrimination or injustice, and miraculously we discover that we can be even more effective in confronting it.

Most of us, as a result of conditioning, have repetitious and predictable responses to the stimuli in our environment. Our reactions seem to be automatically triggered by people and circumstances, and we forget that these are still choices that we are making in every moment of our existence.

DEEPAK CHOPRA

We admit that the practice of the eighth principle of attitudinal healing presents a challenge. If we fail to recognize the rewards—for example our power to choose and the understanding that peace and love *(hedzoleh)* reside with us—we remain stuck. The ability to refocus our attention to be peaceful inside in the midst of fear and conflict is a remarkable achievement. For instance, when we were refused service by the diaper company, we were upset that we were being discriminated against because of the neighborhood we live in. However, we made a choice to focus on peace through dialogue. We were determined to stay peaceful as we dealt with rejection and discrimination. Our goal was to gently demand service and maintain our dignity. As *A Course in Miracles* states, "One of the main purposes of time is to enable us to choose what we want to experience."

Our inner peace can become our daily goal in every moment of the hour; we don't have to wait until a crisis strikes. This is an attitude of peace that can be practiced and strengthened. This attitude of readiness for peace automatically triggers our consciousness to choose peace and be peaceful inside regardless of what is happening. This principle presents the opportunity to exercise our power of choice and reminds us that there is another way, that we do have choice, and that the power to choose can change the old conditioning that makes us react to stimuli with racist thinking.

Marianne's Story

Marianne is another wonderful friend of ours, an Italian woman filled with light and love. In the 1960s she lived in Plainsfield, New Jersey, and she like many of her contemporaries loved Martin Luther King, Jr. and his dream of a world without racism—a world where little black girls and little black boys could play and learn right along with little white girls and boys, a world without violence and fear. She said, "I had that dream, we all had that dream," meaning other young white people. Marianne speaks passionately about her love for a better world. She told us, "I don't know if black people know how devastating it was for some white people when Martin Luther King, Jr. died. It was as if a part of me had died; my dream had died."

For many years Marianne felt left out of the loop as Dr. King's dream faded and the country became more polarized along racial lines. Whites retreated to the suburbs steeped in hopeless and fearful belief that the races could never live in harmony and resigning themselves to the belief that Dr. King's vision was only a dream and could never be a reality.

Marianne shared with us how her first job was teaching in the inner city of Newark, New Jersey. Her aide was also her mentor, a well-connected and respected black woman in Newark. Marianne was teaching in Newark when the riots broke out. She spoke about not ever being afraid to go to work, even though serious fighting was occurring daily in the city.

Mrs. Franklin would call her on certain days to ask her not to go to work, because of the rioting. Marianne would insist on going anyway, thinking that the children relied on her to teach them. Mrs. Franklin would insist that she come to her house first so that she could go to the school with her. Many people were having their cars broken into or damaged in some way by the rioters, but Marianne's car was never destroyed in any manner.

As she looked back on this situation, even though she was not familiar with the principles of attitudinal healing during the 1960s, she told us that she had come to realize she was practicing the eighth principle of attitudinal healing: "We can choose and direct ourselves to be peaceful inside no matter what is happening outside."

Marianne expressed her joy in attending our workshop on racial healing, saying that she now felt heard and validated in having experienced a great loss when Martin Luther King Jr.'s life was taken prematurely. For the first time, she felt that his dream had not died with him. She spoke passionately about Dr. King's dream being renewed through these small group dialogues focused on healing racism. She felt that he would be proud. It has been many years since those days, but she still feels strongly about the dream of Dr. King and she has reclaimed that dream of peace and harmony among the races.

PUTTING PRINCIPLE #8 INTO PRACTICE

"We can choose and direct ourselves to be peaceful inside regardless of what is happening outside."

1. Practice stating the following reminders and affirmations:

145

- I am able to speak up when I hear a racist joke and educate myself and others that there is a better way to communicate about people who appear to be different.

- I acknowledge the power of choice. I will choose in every moment of each day to see differently. I can choose love or fear each moment about each given situation, including those that are racially charged.

- I recognize that I can elect to change negative racial attitudes that hurt. I can choose to learn more about cultures and races other than my own.

- I reclaim my voice. I give voice to peace, love, and non-judgmental acceptance of every living being on earth.

2. Take a few minutes for the next five days and write down your thoughts and feelings as you reflect on each of the following questions. As you journal, keep in mind the thought that you can choose to be peaceful inside no matter what is happening outside.

Day 1: What am I fearful about in my life now because of my belief about other races?

Day 2: What am I not enjoying in my life as a result of my belief about those who are different from me, those who are the "other"?

Day 3: Do I truly love and accept myself to the degree that I am not afraid to share love with other races?

Day 4: What has to happen to keep me centered in love rather than stuck in fear about the "other"?

Day 5: Who are my role models for a more peaceful coexistence with others?

CHAPTER TWELVE

We Are All Learning

You must accept them and accept them with love.
For these innocent people have no other hope.
They are, in effect, still trapped in a history which they
do not understand; and until they understand it,
they cannot be released from it. They have had to believe
for many years, and for innumerable reasons,
that black men are inferior to white men.

JAMES BALDWIN

ATTITUDINAL HEALING PRINCIPLE #9

"We are students and teachers to each other."

Any time we feel superior to another, especially based on racial differences, we are teaching ourselves to judge and evaluate. True peace can never be found through this process. Feeling superior and feeling inferior are two sides of the same coin. They are both based in internalized racism, which is the root of the disease. The notion that one race or tribe is superior rests on a false assumption. A superiority complex closes doors of goodwill and artificially limits us. As Ralph Waldo Emerson once said, "Nature hates monopolies and exceptions."

It seems almost something abnormal
that over a portion of the earth's surface
nature should be nothing and [humanity] everything.

ALBERT SCHWEITZER

That which we are teaching is always teaching us, and in this way we are truly all students and teachers to one another. By holding this truth in our consciousness, we open a door that allows us to learn all that we have learned before. If we truly want to heal ourselves of racism in America, we must consciously bring ideas of unconditional love and oneness in humanity into the center of community as concepts that we willingly teach. In this way, we will learn unconditional love and the oneness of humanity. We cannot overemphasize the importance of *teaching* peace to the process of *learning* peace.

An Impossible Teacher

Some time after I (Aeeshah) first got involved with the work of attitudinal healing and *A Course in Miracles,* I had the good fortune and the intense challenge to spend a summer with Helen Schucman, one of the scribes of *A Course in Miracles.* By that time, in 1980, I was into my fourth year as an avid student of the daily workbook associated with the *Course.* Serious students usually began each year on January 1 with the first lesson from the workbook, with the goal of ending the year's devotional study on December 31.

One day early that summer, Jerry Jampolsky telephoned me to tell me that Helen Schucman was coming out to California for a visit. He went on to share with me that while he was in meditation he had been guided to ask me to stay with Helen while she was vacationing in Tiburon. "Jerry," I told him, "I think you'd better go back to your meditation and look more deeply into this, because I don't think I'm the one to stay with Helen." I went on to say, "To be honest, Jerry, I don't think I can stay with a little old Caucasian lady." Although I was deeply immersed in studying *A Course in Miracles*, I still had one foot in the Nation of Islam.

So Jerry said to me, "Well, Aeeshah, I really hope you won't say no right now. Would you please just pray on it?"

I hung up the telephone with the thought that Jerry was crazy for asking me to stay with Helen, and I would definitely be crazy if I even considered such a task. Even though Helen Schucman was the scribe of *A Course in Miracles*, and even though I dearly loved those books, living with her even for a short period of time seemed out of the question. Besides, my mother had worked hard all her life so that we would not have to clean up after "white folks."

Despite my inner resistance to the idea of living with a little old Caucasian lady, cooking for her, cleaning up after her, and being her companion, when I did my morning prayer, which included an hour in silent meditation, visions kept coming to me that were focused around Helen. I even tried to imagine the possibility that this could be a positive opportunity—after all, this woman had been given the gift of receiving the most powerful spiritual document I had run across. Eventually, I opened *A Course in Miracles* to gain more insight into whether or not I should accept Jerry's offer. The book fell open at the following quote: "Would you not go through fear to love? For such the journey seems to be. Love calls, but hate would have you stay. Hear not the call of hate, and see no fantasies. For your completion lies in truth, and nowhere else. See in the call of hate, and in every fantasy that rises to delay you, but the call for help that rises ceaselessly from you to your Creator. Would He not answer you whose completion is His? He loves you, wholly without illusion, as you must love. For love is wholly without illusion, and therefore wholly without fear."

Finally, I knew that I could not let fear hold me back, even though spending time with Helen felt totally out of my comfort zone. I knew without a doubt that I was meant to go. After a week of deep reflection, I called Jerry and agreed that I would go and spend this time with Helen.

I took time off my job. Making arrangements with my family for me to be gone meant that my husband would take on additional responsibilities. My dear friend Sharifah would take over as a mother for my daughter. Sharifah and I shared in the rearing of our children, which is the way Muslim women build community and sisterhood.

I left to go over to Tiburon, where Helen would be staying. I had some fear about staying in Tiburon, because it was an upper middle-class white community, and was not known as being particularly friendly to people of color, especially poor people of color. In fact, most of its poor people were day help. They came only to do manual labor and day jobs, such as gardening, housekeeping, or cooking.

I soon discovered that Helen was a very difficult woman. She was extremely bright but highly critical and somewhat paranoid. She seemed to be prejudiced against people of color. She was used to having black people serve her, and she automatically assumed that this was my line of work. I tried to tell her about myself and about how I had come to be her caretaker during her visit to California. She immediately cut me short by saying, "I am not interested in what you do. Do you know how to cook low-fat foods? I cannot eat fried foods." I immediately felt shut down. I thought to myself, "How am I going to answer a call for love in this woman?"

My next attempt to connect with Helen was to strike up a conversation about *A Course in Miracles*, thinking that she might be more approachable on this topic. I said to her,

"Helen, I've been a student of *A Course in Miracles* for four years now, and I still have difficulty understanding the section in Chapter 19 on obstacles to peace." She looked at me as if I had called her a bitch and said vehemently, "Aeeshah, if you want to read *A Course in Miracles*, you read it, but under no circumstance are you to bother me with it." In this way, I learned of Helen's intense resistance to talking about *A Course in Miracles* with me. It was very hard for me not to take this rejection personally.

As I began to observe Helen, at first I experienced many judgments about her, and it was very difficult for me to see her light, or essence. To support my process, I would get up very early, do my meditations, prepare Helen's tea, and attempt to move past my judgments.

Among other things, I was still struggling with the Nation of Islam belief that all whites are devils. My struggles with Helen did much to support the beliefs promulgated by the Nation of Islam. During my stay with her, Helen was totally caught up in herself and very critical of everyone around her. It seemed as if instead of my being a companion to Helen, I was there to fight with her. Every day seemed to bring another conflict between us. I could not be the obedient servant Helen was looking for. I was judging her, and she appeared to be judging me. However, our poor relationship did not interfere with the commitment we had made to spend this period of time together. Neither one of us called it quits. As time flew by, our relationship did not get any better, but somehow we managed to push past our judgments about each other.

Eventually things got to the point where Helen would even compliment me on occasion. I remember one afternoon when I was driving her to her doctor's appointment and she remarked, "Aeeshah, you are a pretty good driver." I simply replied, "Yes." I had learned that the best way to avoid an argument with Helen was to agree with her and keep silent.

Helen's husband, Louie, joined her on her vacation. I was surprised by how different he was from Helen. He was an absolute gem, as sweet as apple pie. I often wondered how they ever got connected. By this time, I had truly come to think of Helen as a bitch. Each day we would go through our routine, with me preparing her food, doing the necessary tasks during the day, and preparing for her many guests, who were generally in awe of her as the scribe of *A Course in Miracles*. I would sit quietly observing their visits, noting that Helen was very polite to them. She allowed them to raise questions about the *Course* and on occasion even answered them.

These guests were all white, and I wondered to myself, "Is Helen a racist?" But as soon as the people would leave, Helen would turn to me and ask, "What is wrong with those people? Why do they come? If they want to read these books, why don't they just read them? Why do they have to bother me with them? What are they looking for?" And I would look back at Helen and ask disdainfully, "Helen, why are you asking me? You know why they are coming. They are coming because they want to connect with the scribe of *A Course in Miracles*." She would look at me and say, "I am not interested in them," and I would reply, "Too bad; they are interested in you."

As I look back on that time, I can see how much I've grown. Back then, I did not see Helen as an elderly Jewish woman. I just saw her as a little old Caucasian lady. I did not think of her in terms of her life as a Jewish woman born in New York before World War I or that she had survived seeing her fellow Jews dying in the millions during the European Holocaust. Helen had led a very sheltered life with a privileged childhood including servants, a cook, and a governess.

I did not think of Helen as Jewish, because growing up in the South, you were either white or black. Other ethnic groups did not count. Whatever their ethnicity, white people in the South became as white as they could be. So in meeting Helen, all I thought about was that she was just another elderly white woman. By the time I met her, she was seventy-one years old. She was very frail and physically ill. Despite her fragility, she was stubborn as a mule, highly opinionated, and extremely difficult to live with peacefully.

Notwithstanding our difficulties, we kept to our commitment. I felt the strain of our relationship, because every day that I spent with Helen, I had to work on my perception of her. My challenge was getting past all my judgments about her so that I could see her goodness. I was not feeling very successful at this. Helen's vacation was coming to a close, and our time together was coming to an end. Finally, it was our last day together. We went to Jerry Jampolsky's for a goodbye lunch. I was thinking to myself how glad I was that my commitment to be a companion to Helen had come to an end; I felt good about having honored it, but it had been hell. I stood on Jerry's balcony overlooking the bay, thinking about how happy I was to be going home, where I would be rid of Helen. While I was standing there thinking this, Helen joined me on the balcony. She looked at me and I looked at her, and she put her hands on my shoulder. As she looked deeply into my eyes, for a moment we were lost in each other. For that moment, I could not tell where Helen ended and I began.

Helen said to me, "Aeeshah, I know that I have not helped you much with your belief that Caucasians are devils, have I?"

As she said this to me, I knew instantly and without a doubt what the truth was. I looked at her and said, "Helen, it's not your responsibility. It's mine. It is my responsibility to shift my perception. But I want to thank you for what you are saying to me today."

So we parted, and Helen went back to New York. I didn't realize it then, but that was the last time I would see Helen. By the following February, she had passed away.

Sometime after, in the summer of 1982, I came home and found some mail from Judy Skutch-Whitson, the president of the Foundation for Inner Peace, which publishes *A Course in Miracles*. The package contained a book entitled *The Gifts of God* by Helen Schucman. As I turned the pages, I was very touched to read about Helen's life and the inner dictation that took place over ten years and resulted in *A Course in Miracles*. This book helped me understand Helen on a deeper level, and in turn I gained insight into my process with Helen. The most valuable lesson I learned from Helen was to rely on my inner guidance. She taught me that the only guru we need is the teacher within.

Helen best described her process in receiving *A Course in Miracles* in the introduction to her book of poetry, *The Gifts of God:* "It made me very uncomfortable, but it never seriously occurred to me to stop. It seemed to be a special assignment I had somehow, somewhere agreed to complete. It represented a truly collaborative venture between Bill and myself, and much of its significance, I am sure, lies in that. I could neither account for nor reconcile my obviously inconsistent attitudes. On the one hand I still regarded myself as officially an agnostic, resented the material I was taking down, and was strongly impelled to attack it and prove it wrong. On the other hand I spent considerable time in taking it down and later in dictating it to Bill, so it was apparent that I took it quite seriously. I actually came to refer to it as my life's work. As Bill pointed out, I must believe in it if only because I argued with it so much. While this was true, it did not help me. I was in the impossible position of not believing in my own life's work. The situation was clearly ridiculous as well as painful."

As I opened my heart and read her story and perused her poetry, it became clear to me that despite her doubts, Helen loved her work and knew the part she was to play. As I read the poem "The Ancient Love" from *The Gifts of God,* I felt it described my experience with her:

The Ancient Love

Love, You are silent. Not one shining word
Has reached my heart for an eternity
Of waiting and of tears. I have forgot
Your face that once was everything to me,
But now is almost nothing. What You were
I do but half remember. What You are
I do not know at all. What You will be
Is unimagined. Sometimes I believe
I knew You once. And then again I think
You were a dream that once I thought was real.

My eyes are closing, Love. Without Your Word
I will but sleep, and sleeping will forget
Even the dream. Is silence what You gave
In golden promise as the Son of God?
Is this bleak unresponsive shadowland
The overcoming that You offered those
Who understood the Father through the Son?
Is endless distance what must stand between
My Love and me? You promised that You will
Forever answer. Yet, Love, You are still.

HELEN SCHUCMAN

After reading Helen's poem I thought again about her statement that she hadn't helped me shift my belief about Caucasians. I realized that whenever we see another human being as intolerant, critical, angry, prejudiced, or hateful, what we're really seeing is a human being who is asleep to love, who doesn't remember. I began to experience Helen in a whole different way, and truly acknowledge what a teacher she had been to me. Helen taught me the power of choice; she taught me that I could choose to practice the principles in *A Course in Miracles* because I found value in them. I also learned to appreciate the fact that Helen wasn't some holy guru on high, nor was she a demon filled with evil, but simply a human being like me, who came to teach me about finding my own way, who came to teach me about forgiveness. With all of her personality flaws, Helen created opportunities for people all over the world to do the work for ourselves. As I began to heal my attitude about interpretations and judgments, I saw that I did indeed have the power of choice, and that I could choose to embrace the truth that the essence of our being is love.

An African Boy

I (Aeeshah) am constantly learning that age is no factor when it comes to receiving teaching. While I was traveling in Ghana, West Africa, recently, one of my most powerful teachers was a four-year-old boy. We had just arrived in Ghana and were staying in Kokomon's family compound in Abossey Okai. The first few days we spent resting and meeting Kokomon's many family members. We had come home during the Homowo season, which is the time of festivals and harvest celebrations for many of the tribes indigenous to the coastal villages of Ghana.

Kokomon planned to join with his brothers and sisters to give his father an eightieth birthday party. It was a grand time for everyone. Libations had been poured and the ancestors called to bless all the events of the family. All of Kokomon's brothers had been summoned home. His brother from the Ivory Coast was on his way, and his younger brother who had been living in Europe with his white European wife and new baby boy had just arrived. They had planned all kinds of family celebrations. I would also get to witness an outdooring-naming ritual, the traditional welcoming ceremony for the new baby from Europe. I was quite entranced with all the excitement and air of festivities.

Two days before the big birthday party, I was in the family compound enjoying myself with all the children—both those who lived in the compound as well as the many who were visiting with their parents. The children were determined to teach me a few Ga words, such as "Te oyor teh," which means "How are you?"

That same day, I met Atukwei, a wonderful young boy of four years. He asked me immediately, "Where are you from?" I was excited that he was showing an interest in me.

Atukwei was the youngest son of one of Kokomon's older brothers who lived in the city of Accra. The very next day, I met Atukwei's mother. She came over to me as soon as she entered the family compound. She introduced herself. Her name was Amelia. Amelia looked at me curiously and said, "I came to meet you." She went on to say that Atukwei had come home all excited the day before, saying to her, "Mom, there are two white women in the family house, and one had white skin and the other had black skin." I was a little taken aback, because I wondered whether the little boy was calling me a white woman with black skin. Atukwei's mother went on to say that she had stopped everything to come to the family's compound, even though she had not planned to come over until the day of the Old Man's birthday party. She was referring to Kokomon's father as the Old Man—a term of endearment for him as the head of the family.

I was stunned and somewhat angered by the idea that I had been presented with a four-year-old's notion of who I am. I immediately became defensive, saying, "I am not a white woman." I was thinking to myself, "I haven't traveled fifteen thousand miles to the homeland that I have always dreamed of returning to visit only to be called a white woman!" This was the ultimate insult. How was I going to let this go?

It took me about two weeks of my month-long stay in Ghana to come to a place of peace with this encounter. I felt defensive many times when I was in conversation with the people I was meeting in Ghana. I wanted to clarify for them that I was not a white woman but a member of the African Diaspora who happened to live in America. I would find myself giving lengthy explanations about being an African American, even before an inquiry was made. One day, as I was beginning to explain who I was to a woman in the marketplace, it dawned on me that it did not matter—who I really was lay beyond any explanation I could give in a few words. It also dawned on me that little Atukwei had given me a gift—the gift of looking beyond form. This young boy had tapped into my energy and that of the other Western woman in the family compound, and he had called our Western European energy white. I was challenged to look past form into content. I was challenged to truly stand on the ground of understanding that the essence of our being is love.

Both Teachers and Students

One of the things that's really valuable about attitudinal healing work is beginning to see how we're all students and teachers to one another. We can learn to be sensitive when our roles reverse, because many times we have observed that the things we're teaching to others are actually teaching us. So often our students are actually teaching us; they are truly our teachers. When we remain open and receptive to these shifts in roles, we open ourselves up to ever greater learning.

Sometimes we find that when we think we're the student we're really the teacher, and when we think we're teaching, we are really learning. The roles change and fluctuate. Recognizing this is ultimate freedom. We no longer have to try to control the process. We come to recognize the absolute and fundamental equality of each and every one of us. Racism simply cannot coexist with this awareness.

When we accept the fact that we are not superior to the "other," no matter how we define the "other," we have started on the long road to healing. Attitudes of superiority or inferiority can be addictive. We can come to rely on these types of attitudes like drugs. This principle opens us to the possibility that we can learn from all situations and all people. It offers us the opportunity to be open-minded and open-hearted in the face of new experiences and new possibilities.

In Ghana, West Africa, we observed that this principle is extremely challenging for the elders as well as the young. In Ghana, it is the belief that the elders have all the answers to all the problems facing the village, and this belief creates a system of protocol based on age. This is so entrenched in everyone's consciousness that it creates separation. At our recent attitudinal healing training in Ghana, West Africa, the ninth principle was very popular among the young. It is culturally unacceptable for young people to share information with their elders. This is considered disrespectful. Many of the young people spoke of their need to share more fully with their elders and were very excited to have an opportunity to dialogue openly with them. Conversely, the elders were delighted to step out of the role of knowing it all; they willingly created a space and time for heart-to-heart dialogue.

Every circumstance at every moment presents a classroom, an opportunity to either teach or be taught. Gaining new insight on this principle offers a remarkable step toward healing this disease we call racism. In this light, a dialogue that includes all the ethnic groups would offer an opportunity for all groups to learn from one another. One of the first things we do when we want to shift the way we see the "other" is to consciously go among the "other" with the single goal of being a student in the process of learning.

PUTTING PRINCIPLE #9 INTO PRACTICE

"We are students and teachers to each other."

1. In any situation concerned with race, ask yourself: What role am I playing? Am I the teacher or the student? If you are not sure, listen deeply for some clues as to what it is you might be learning in the situation you are in now. What might you be teaching? Notice carefully at what point your role changes.

2. State to yourself this intention: Today I will commit myself to being aware of my role as student or teacher as it relates to fear of those of different racial or ethnic groups.

3. Write about three different interactions in which you played the role of teacher or student with regard to your awareness about racism.

4. Examine what inferiority complexes you carry. Examine your superiority complexes. Write about your observations.

5. Write about three attributes you have that you would like to share with someone whom you see as the "other." What three things would you like to learn from those of other cultures?

CHAPTER THIRTEEN

Focusing on the Whole

*The ecological fact is well known, that diversity of species
in an ecosystem leads to resilience; an ecosystem consisting
primarily of one species is fragile, susceptible to being wiped out
by disease or invasion. Similarly, human society on earth is
more resilient for being comprised of many diverse cultures.*

WILLIS HARMAN

ATTITUDINAL HEALING PRINCIPLE #10

"We can focus on the whole of life rather than the fragments."

When we focus on the whole of life rather than the fragments, we begin to see the whole picture and how everything
works together for the good of all humanity. We can begin to
see the little parts that each of us plays.

Many of us only experience a vague sense of the wholeness of vision called for by the tenth principle of attitudinal
healing, because we are so accustomed to focusing on the
fragments. The phrase *the whole of life* means all existing
things, including the earth and all its creatures, the heavenly
bodies, and everything else throughout space. Focusing on the
whole of life awakens us to one fundamental truth: That is,
we are connected to all people whether we like it or not.
Thus, we are compelled to face this truth: All things are in-
terdependent and inseparable parts of this cosmic whole—
different manifestations of the same ultimate reality.

Focusing on the Whole

The wholeness of life has, from of old,
been made manifest in its parts.

LAO-TZU

An African Story

The following story, which Kokomon learned growing up in Ghana, speaks of how easily we can fall into defining ourselves as a group separate from others, even in the face of the most glaring similarities:

Once upon a time, in Korleyman, an African village, two rains had not come, and many of the savanna's waterholes had dried into mud. The days of hunger had begun. Everyone in the village—all the people and all the animals—offered prayers and sacrifices, asking that Onyami (God) spare them all from starvation.

Suddenly, the hot skies clouded over, the light breezes became brisk winds, and the little rains began, falling warmly as always. The little rains became big rains, and all the animals took shelter, listening to the water pounding on the thatch roofs, with lightning flashing and thunder rumbling.

After the rains had subsided, Mrs. Chicken hurried and assembled all of her seven chicks in the compound full of mud to search for food. It was not long before the little chicks began to feel cold, and they asked their mother to take them back inside their thatched hut. Mrs. Chicken gathered them all under her wings for shelter, but that did not protect the chicks from the cold air.

"We are cold with fever," the chicks told their mother.

"Don't worry," Mrs. Chicken told them. "I will cook you some chicken soup with ginger root to take your fever away."

"Chicken!?" the chicks questioned in chorus.

"Don't worry," said Mrs. Chicken. "It won't be one of us!"

The message of the story is clear: We humans deceive ourselves into thinking that so long as it's not "one of us," it's okay for us to kill and do whatever we please, ignoring the deeper truth that in reality we're all part of the same whole, and no one can be excluded.

There is a story in the Bible with a similar message. In his letter to the Corinthians, Paul writes:

For as the body is one and has many members, and all the
members of the body, though many, are one body, so it is with
Christ. For by one Spirit we were all baptized into one body—
Jews or Greeks, slaves or free—and all were made to drink of
one Spirit. For the body does not consist of one member but
of many. If the foot should say, "Because I am not a hand, I
do not belong to the body," that would not make it any less
a part of the body. And if the ear should say, "Because I am
not an eye, I do not belong to the body," that would not make
it any less a part of the body. If the whole body were an eye,
where would be the hearing? If the whole body were an
ear, where would be the sense of smell? But as it is, God
arranged the organs in the body, each one of them, as he
chose. If all were a single organ, where would the body be?
As it is, there are many parts, yet one body. The eye cannot
say to the hand, "I have no need of you," nor again the head
to the feet, "I have no need of you." On the contrary, the parts
of the body which seem to be weaker are indispensable, and
those parts of the body which we think less honorable we
invest with the greater honor, and our unpresentable parts
are treated with greater modesty, which our more presentable
parts do not require. But God has so adjusted the body, giving
the greater honor to the inferior part, that there may be no
discord in the body, but that the members may have the same

164

care for one another. If one member suffers, all suffer
together; if one member is honored, all rejoice together.

1 Corinthians 12:12-26

This passage offers a profound reminder of the intercon-nection of all humanity, for truly we are members of one body, all indispensable. We humans are like the ignorant eye that does not think it needs a hand. But the truth is that all members of the human family are needed and important. When each member of the body comes to recognize the pur-pose of the other members, and the truth that they are part of one whole, they are joined, and healing is present.

So it is with racism—we experience the false sense of divi-sion and separation. One of the first steps in the process of healing racism is diversity awareness: We become willing to recognize and understand other cultures and to develop tol-erance for both differences and similarities. This is only the first step, however, because the underlying message is "I can tolerate you, but I cannot love you as my brother or sister." The next step is personal racial healing and includes the es-sential recognition that racism is spiritual deprivation. At this point, we approach the realm of universal kinship, with the deep understanding of a key spiritual truth: "The essence of our being is love."

Chinese Take-Out

One day I (Aeeshah) came home from work, and my daughter wanted some Chinese food for dinner. On my way home, I had noticed that a new local Chinese restaurant had opened, just on the corner from where we lived, so we could easily walk there. I was relieved at my daughter's suggestion, since I wasn't in the mood to drive anywhere. So we walked

165

to the corner, and I told her I'd like to get take-out, because I wasn't in the mood for sitting in a restaurant for a long time.

When we got in the restaurant, I sat down, and when a waitress passed me, I waved her down, and I immediately told her, "I'd like to get an order of food to go please."

"One moment," she said. She left and didn't come back right away, and I sat there for a few more minutes.

Then a young waiter passed by, and I waved him down and repeated that I wanted to get an order of food to go. He also said, "One moment," then left and didn't come back.

I sat there awhile, and then I noticed another young woman up at the counter, so I got up and approached her. This was a nice-sized restaurant, around eleven hundred square feet with a counter in the back with the cash register, where you could get food to go. It was dinnertime, and there were quite a few people in the restaurant eating their dinner. As I walked back toward the counter, I noticed the first waitress I had spoken with, and I reminded her that I wanted to get an order of food to go. I was getting a little concerned. I wasn't in a big hurry, but I knew I didn't want to eat in the restaurant; I just wanted to get the food and go home. Again the young woman said, "One moment," and she went in the back. Once again, she didn't take our order.

I was wondering what was going on when an elderly woman came out of the back of the restaurant. I was pleased at first, thinking that now I was going to get some service. So I immediately started to give her my order, asking for rice with prawns, but then I noticed that she wasn't writing anything down. She looked at me and said, "I'm sorry; we don't serve you people."

As she said this, I looked closely at her, and rather than get upset and heap abuses on her, I got very close to her, looked deeply into her eyes, and held her hand as I said, "You know, you have a choice, and I want to share with you that you don't have to serve me, but I want you to understand the kind of example that you are setting for the young people who work in this restaurant. And I want you to know that there are all kinds of people in the world. There are good black people and bad black people, good white people and bad white people, good Chinese people and bad Chinese people, and you can choose how you want to connect with people around this. You can choose who you will serve and who you will not serve, but to serve or not to serve according to race— well, I just feel like you're not really thinking about the choice you're making right now and the role that you're modeling for the young people working here with you. Now I know you don't know me and I don't know you, but I just feel that it's important for me to share this with you right now."

As I looked into her eyes and listened to her accent, I recognized that she had not been born in this country. She had a perception of me as a black person, and my skin color had a negative connotation for her. I certainly knew that many times black people are given a very negative reputation in this society. The media paint black people very negatively, and if we look in the dictionary we find that black connotes evil. Young black boys are depicted as violent. So I was aware of all this as I looked in her eyes, and after a moment or two I just dropped her hand and thanked her.

My daughter was looking at me with awe at that moment. At that very moment as we were being rejected and refused service, we weren't feeling rejected or victimized. We didn't take on the role of being victims. We just looked at this woman and we honored her. I just stood there, not quite believing I had spoken in this way to this woman, and she was equally awed because she clearly was listening intently to every word that came out of my mouth. As I was releasing her hand, both she and I felt the release.

As my daughter and I stepped back and began to walk out of the restaurant, I could hear a voice behind me saying, "Ma'am, please, come back; we'll serve you."

Now at this point a part of me was feeling separate, and I did not want her to serve me. This was just a part of me—a part of me that saw her as the "other," someone who was offensive and cruel, someone to stay far away from. But just as my separated self was beginning to come into play, and deny the joining of a moment, my daughter looked at me and said, "Mom, I'm hungry."

So rather than getting stuck in a place of separation over the situation and stepping out of the process of what had happened, I listened to my daughter, who was reminding me to be practical. And I thought about the biblical saying, "And a little child shall lead them." So we stayed and got our Chinese take-out.

I reflected later on the changing roles of teacher and student that we all play for one another. I believe the elderly Chinese woman learned something from me, but I also learned something about the power of speaking the truth from my heart. And I learned, too, that my young daughter possessed a wisdom that could reawaken my own connection with my heart, reminding me of the power of forgiveness.

Sometimes our egos as adults get so full we can't seem to let go and be humble and step aside and forgive. Our hearts grow hard, but attitudinal healing has the power to soften hearts. I believe that it is through the softening of the heart that we heal, and through this softening we begin to take the kinds of steps in the world that can help others soften, too.

As I look back at the experience in the Chinese restaurant, I recognize that it could have developed into a very ugly incident, but instead, because I practiced the principles of attitudinal healing, it turned into an experience that brought people together. I remember thinking that the elderly woman could have been my daughter's grandmother, and I felt bound to honor this age factor. I also remembered that as an African American my ancestors have been here for generations—we are truly an American-made product, and our connections are so totally here that when we think of going to another country, even in Africa, it is truly foreign to us.

I recognized that the woman at the Chinese restaurant had come to this country and adopted the beliefs of the wider society, and the wider society believes that blacks are throwaway people, the children of slaves, lazy and shiftless, and undeserving of service. These are the kinds of perceptions that many people who come into this country receive about African Americans. Somehow as I reflected on this, compassion stepped in and helped me to choose again. As *A Course in Miracles* states: "Trials are but lessons that you failed to learn presented once again, for where you made a faulty choice before you now can make a better one and thus escape all pain that what you chose before has brought to you, and with every difficulty, all distress, and each perplexity, Christ calls to you and gently says, 'My brother [sister], choose again.'"

Truly, when you think about this country and all the opportunities it has to correct its mistakes, you can see that racism has indeed been like a curse. The work to heal racism, then, is blessed work. It is through learning to face our fears and let go of them, face our feelings and move past them, examine our perceptions and correct them, that we begin to be able to carry on a cross-cultural dialogue, an honest exchange of feelings. This is where true racial healing becomes possible. Part of the process is self-acceptance, and as we work with each principle of attitudinal healing and make it our own, we will truly experience that the essence of our being is love. This is what the work of racial healing brings us to—the center and the core of our being.

As I share with you the story of going to the Chinese restaurant with my daughter and being refused service, part of me knows that I can never be refused. A part of me knew during the experience itself that it is only through joining and connecting with other people, and recognizing that I wasn't being attacked, that healing can enter. Some part of me knew that this elderly woman would never attack me and if she had known what she was doing, she wouldn't have been doing it. I saw her with compassion, as my sister. I saw the whole of the situation rather than the fragments.

Recognizing Wholeness

This notion of interdependence and inseparability requires that we commit ourselves to healing racism and bridging the gap between all races. Wholeness and connection can sometimes manifest in ways that we would not have imagined. We have an acquaintance who was very proud of her WASP heritage. She was constantly talking about her family and their English connection. As a matter of fact, she claimed that her family had come over on the *Mayflower*. During one conversation with us, she explained that she had been doing a genealogy study on her family and recently discovered that there is some African blood in her lineage. She was somewhat distraught over the issues this had raised for her. As she shared this information, we listened with love to her story.

Even though she wasn't particularly joyful over her discovery, our friend ended her sharing by saying that we are all related somehow. She was beginning to understand the tenth principle of attitudinal healing.

PUTTING PRINCIPLE #10 INTO PRACTICE

"We can focus on the whole of life rather than the fragments."

1. Repeat to yourself the following statements. Let them into your heart.

-   The air that I breathe is the same air that all humanity is breathing right now. We all breathe the same air.

-   My basic needs for air, food, water, shelter, and clothing are shared by all humanity.

-   The peace and love and happiness that I desire every moment are desired by all humanity.

-   My intention to focus on the whole of life will enhance my relationship with all people.

-   Today, my intention is to embrace all humanity. I am open to experiencing peace, love, and happiness to the degree that I share peace, love, and happiness with people of all races and backgrounds.

-   I release my attitudes of racial intolerance and surrender to the belief that I can accept and give love and affection to all regardless of race, creed, or color.

2. To practice the tenth principle of attitudinal healing, write a list of particular groups or races that you have difficulty accepting. You may even admit to yourself that

you hate these groups of people. Whenever you think of or see people from these groups, silently say to your-self, I honor and respect the fabric that you are made of in the spirit of brotherhood and sisterhood. I love you as myself. Each day, allow your intention to grow to accept the wholeness of life.

CHAPTER FOURTEEN

Love Is Eternal

The Cosmic Dancer, declares Nietzsche,
does not rest heavily in a single spot,
but gaily, lightly, turns and leaps
from one position to another.

JOSEPH CAMPBELL

ATTITUDINAL HEALING PRINCIPLE #11

"Since love is eternal,
death need not be viewed as fearful."

Sara's Story

I (Aeeshah) had a friend I'll call Sara, and I've always found it hard to accept the tremendous pain she was in. I wanted to help her, but I finally had to realize that there are some things beyond my power to fix. Sara was an American of darker hue, an American of African descent who grew up in the South.

She sometimes talked about the pain of seeing her own mother working in the home of a white family, and spending more time taking care of the white family's children than her own. Sara's dream was to get as far away as she could from the South and everything black. Her dream was to work in corporate America, so she earned her college degree and pursued that goal.

I remember the first time she came to our center in West Oakland. It was hard for her. Now, perception is everything, and I love West Oakland and look at it as one of the best kept secrets in America—we have the best weather and sunshine in the Bay Area, easy access to the freeways, and a strong community—but to Sara, living in a predominantly black community meant there was something wrong with you. She was really afraid even to come to participate in the Healing Racism Circle at our center.

Sara had done so much to be accepted by the corporate world: She had gone to the right schools, worked hard to get the right grades, wore the right clothes for the corporate look, and did everything she felt would get her accepted by her peers. But she was experiencing tremendous pain, because no matter how hard she worked, she still did not feel accepted by others. I remember her talking about going to a Christmas party. She forced her husband to spend huge amounts of money on a new suit and new shoes, and she spent a lot on new clothes for herself, too, because she wanted to impress her co-workers so they would finally accept her.

My heart went out to Sara, because it was so clear that unless she accepted herself, there was no way anyone else could fill her emptiness. Because she was black, Sara felt others would never accept her. I wondered if it was because she was black that she would never accept herself.

As time passed and our relationship developed, I raised some of these issues, but I wasn't sure if I was getting through, or if she really heard what I was saying. I had to recognize that I couldn't really change her; this was a lesson for me, too, about acceptance.

After the Christmas party, things seemed to get progressively worse for Sara. She was having difficulties in her relationship with her peers at work, and when the company started to downsize, she was quite fearful she would lose her job. She was so fearful that instead of waiting to see what would happen, she gave her notice. She was in tremendous pain over this, and felt there was no way she could win.

Sara's life showed the devastating effects of what internalized racism can do to a person. Sara was so fearful of not being accepted, so terrified of being rejected and being hated because her skin was black that she made the move to quit even before they let her go. "I will reject you before you reject me" was her stance.

Throughout this period, I was learning just to listen to Sara and accept totally where she was. A couple of weeks went by, and I didn't hear from her. Then one morning, two days before what was to be Sara's last day at work, I got a phone call from a mutual friend saying that our friend had shot herself in the head.

I was absolutely devastated. It was two months before the Healing Racism Workshop that I had invited her to attend. I went to the hospital, and she was in a coma. I was not at all prepared for this, and I began to deal with the consequences of her action and think about the pain that her internalized racism had caused, reminding me once again that racism is a life-threatening disease.

Some of her other friends and I visited her often at the hospital. It wasn't clear if she would recover or not. When the Healing Racism Workshop finally happened, we placed her in the circle. She couldn't be physically present, but we placed her energy in the circle, for she represented to all of us the kind of pain one can inflict upon one's self as a result of internalized racism.

As I reflect back on Sara's action, it still horrifies me to think of this beautiful, talented, extremely wonderful, and awesome human being, taking a gun and holding it to her head and trying to blow her brains out. It's catastrophic. She lived with such pain that she was choosing to die. My heart went out to her as I thought of the negative images she had absorbed from our society. This experience confirmed in me the belief that we must begin to tap into the essence of who we really are if we are to move beyond the cycle of racist conditioning.

One day I went to visit Sara and as I sat at her bedside I talked to her and let her know that we had brought her into the circle at the Healing Racism Workshop that day, and that when we brought her into the circle, we wanted her to know that we had all joined with her in letting go of the internalized racism that she had connected with when she hurt herself. At that moment, as I shared with her about including her in our circle, she turned and opened her eyes and looked at me for the first time in all those months that she had been lying there in a coma in intensive care. In that moment, I looked into her eyes, and she held my hand but did not say a word to me. It was as if she felt the love of those of us who had joined together. Then she turned around and closed her eyes again. We left there that day feeling very connected and much more aware that we're not these bodies we think we are—that we're so much more.

In that moment, I knew that we are all born completely free from all prejudice and racism and that we are all inherently good and noble people. We are born open and responsible and clear thinking, seeking knowledge and connection to others because that is our reality. In reality we are all one. We are all connected. Humanity is one.

As time passed, Sara began to heal and reclaim her health, and one day the phone rang, and my dear friend said, "Hello," with the voice that I knew when I first met her, a joyful voice. She asked me if I had time to talk, and I was thrilled. It was Thanksgiving Day—that was the beauty of it—not Thanksgiving

Day in the sense of November 27 but Thanksgiving Day in the beauty of the thanksgiving we must have when we reach into a place of healing past painful situations. The phone call I got from Sara that day spoke to the kind of thanksgiving we feel when we are able to turn a painful experience into an opportunity.

Sara told me that when she was in the coma, she had a round-table discussion with God. She had a meeting with God, and in that meeting God told her that she had tried to leave here, but it wasn't her time yet, that she needed to return. God told her that she would be able to return with assistance and support and healing, and she had to return because her work wasn't finished. She had to share her story. And as I'm sharing this story with you the reading audience, I hope you'll understand the power of Sara's meeting with God.

I realized that when Sara had been in the coma, and all the while she was unconscious, there was a part of her that was alive and active and well and strong and beautiful and unique. The truth of her being had been having a meeting with a higher being.

We all have that same capacity to call a meeting with the part of us that is all-knowing, the part of us that is love. Since love is eternal, death need not be viewed as fearful. And as my dear friend shared with me her meeting with God, in that moment both she and I knew that death was no escape from the lessons we had to learn and that in truth we all will do the work we have to do on this plane whether we're in a body or out of a body. Sometimes the body is needed, and so Sara had to return to her body, but it was a choice. She had to agree to it. It's not that she was forced; she was given a choice, and she agreed in her meeting with God to return to do her work.

And now, as I'm writing this story, Sara is acting as one of the founders of the Healing Racism Institutes doing work in

California, and to this day I know that her work is grounded in her essence, which is love. Physically, she did not regain all the abilities she once had because of her injuries, but her heart and her mind are at peace with her choices. One of the most important things that my friend feels she learned from her experience is to love herself and not to seek outside of herself for love. She learned to remember who we really are—love.

Healing Our Relationships
Through True Understanding

In his "Mini Course for Healing Relationships and Bringing About Peace of Mind," Jerry Jampolsky reminds us that our perception is a mirror, not a reality.

The eleventh attitudinal healing principle offers a profound message if we truly understand it. It focuses on the wholeness of life. It can be restated in this way: God is love, love is eternal, and transient creations are not of God. Many of us have been raised to believe that the best strategy for dealing with enemies is to exterminate them. We forget the fundamental truth that there is no way to get rid of enemies. The very problem that we think we are exterminating will simply surface in another form.

If we truly believed that love is eternal, we would heal our relationships rather than kill the perceived enemy. We would eliminate the desire to attack ourselves or anyone else when difficult issues surface. We would understand that unless we heal through love, the same problems will keep reemerging.

For example, when our friend Sara attempted to take her life because she was not getting the love and respect she deserved, assume she had succeeded. Would her co-workers have changed overnight and rid themselves of racial prejudice and bias? Consider the recent "ethnic cleansings" that have taken place in Bosnia and Rwanda, the kind of "attitudinal killing" that concludes that exterminating people is the way to resolve fears of the "other." These kinds of actions are devastating to human relationships. Neither genocide nor suicide is the remedy for hatred. In the Ga Tribe of Ghana, West Africa, suicide is not considered an acceptable remedy for any reason. The Ga people practice the belief that life lives on.

God is love, and love is eternal. The saying that human beings are created in the likeness and image of God is equivalent to saying that our essence, which is love, is eternal. Understanding this fact of life releases and frees us from entertaining such insane thoughts as "killing the enemy."

The eleventh principle encourages us to look into our ancestral past. In America, we have not spent much time exploring our past with any depth. Instead, we bury the past, not realizing that it sprouts in the present in ways we do not anticipate. Many of the stories related to the pain we have endured as Americans have been buried, and we live with the guilt of our painful past. Let us explore the past with the goal of healing, so that we can finally be free of the guilt, pain, and rage of our collective histories. In this way, we can face our own deaths with equanimity and a peaceful understanding of the part of us that is eternal.

PUTTING PRINCIPLE #11 INTO PRACTICE

"Since love is eternal, death need not be viewed as fearful."

1. Take an inventory of your life to reveal any residues of hatred. Pay special attention to any prejudices or

biases you may still harbor that are based on racial dif-ferences. Is there anyone in your life whom you have not forgiven? Is there any group of people that you still view negatively?

2. Ask yourself how you are contributing to life as a whole, through giving, serving, or nurturing yourself or someone else. Attitudinal healing suggests that when-ever you are in physical or mental pain, you can find someone to serve. This experience of your essence pro-vides a way to feel relief and find healing from this mal-ady. This is especially true with regard to the disease of racism. When you notice old remnants of prejudice against a particular group, make a point to go out of your way to do something positive for a member of that group.

3. Take an inventory of your ancestors. How were they involved in race relations? Is there anything you would like to release for them? How can you bring them into your process of forgiveness? Ancestral healing is a key way to release ourselves from past hurts.

4. Spend a day socializing with people you view as dif-ferent from yourself.

5. As soon as you awake in the morning, say to your-self that you will look for the good in everyone you meet, especially those of different racial, ethnic, or reli-gious backgrounds. Practice looking for the good in all people throughout the day. In the evening, take an inventory of your efforts for that day. Remember to be gentle with yourself as you work to incorporate new ways of seeing people.

6. What are you willing to eliminate in your beliefs about the "other"? Make a list of the stereotypes that you hold about people of different races. Which of these beliefs could you let go of today?

7. Practice the meditation for healing your ancestors if you have a relative who was bound by racism, either as a victim or as a perpetrator. Take thirty minutes to do this healing ritual at a setting of your choice: a garden, beach, or perhaps a room that your relative actually occupied. Any setting you choose is suitable. Visualize yourself sitting quietly with your relative. Take a few minutes to breathe in the essence of this experience. Now say, "I know that you feel pain because of the hurts that were inflicted upon you or the hurts that you inflicted upon others. I came today because I have realized that we can be free of all past hurts, and I know that I cannot be free without you being free." As you are saying these words, visualize a golden light surrounding you and your ancestor. Feel the warmth of this light. Take a few minutes to allow this light to cleanse you and your ancestor of all pain, guilt, rage, and fears concerning past hurts. Now say to your ancestor, "We are free together. May you walk through the ages lighter and more peaceful, because we have been forgiven together."

CHAPTER FIFTEEN

The Power of Perception

This morning I look through your anguish
Right down to your soul.
I know that with each other,
We can make ourselves whole.

MAYA ANGELOU

ATTITUDINAL HEALING PRINCIPLE #12

"We can always perceive ourselves and others as either extending love or giving a call for help."

In our personal journey, we have found that one of the most challenging tasks is balancing inner experience with outer experience. Perhaps you have found that an interaction with a co-worker, friend, or even stranger has landed you into a conflicted racial situation. We cannot guarantee that the twelfth principle of attitudinal healing will enable you to change this dynamic altogether, but we encourage you to open a space in your heart and mind to ask for help to see differently.

The O. J. Simpson Verdict

Before we can heal ourselves of the wound of racism, we must first bring the wounding to light and face it for what it is. Current events often provide a lens that helps us focus on an issue that is otherwise too painful to look at closely. Few events in recent years have expressed the deep divisions along racial lines more starkly than the murders of Nicole Brown Simpson and Ronald Goldman and the reactions to the O. J. Simpson trial. Let me (Aeeshah) share with you some of my thoughts and experiences around this issue.

At the beginning of October 1995, I boarded a plane on my way to a statewide Mental Health Institute in Louisville, Kentucky. I have traveled to many places in this country, but I had never been to Kentucky. I knew that it was known as the Blue Grass State, renowned for its famous horse race, the Kentucky Derby.

I had been invited to do a workshop on attitudinal healing as a ground of being for working effectively with people who are mentally challenged. For many years now I have worked in mental health, and I have found the principles of attitudinal healing to be essential to this work.

When my plane arrived in Chicago's O'Hare airport in the late afternoon, and I grabbed my carry-on luggage to catch the next plane to Louisville, I noticed something extraordinary in the terminal. Everyone's attention seemed intently focused on watching the televisions mounted in the seating areas. As I noticed the travelers' deep engagement, I immediately realized that it was the O. J. trial. I had totally forgotten about it, or maybe I was choosing to forget about it. It seemed as if the whole world had been hypnotized by the O. J. case since June of 1994. I sat as far away from the CNN outlet as I could get while I waited to board the plane on to my destination. Although the trial had brought the deeply buried issue of race to the front page of every newspaper, over the months that the trial had aired, I had distanced myself emotionally from it. I wasn't sure why.

As I sat there, I couldn't manage to keep my thoughts off the Simpson trial despite my best efforts. My mind drifted, and

I allowed myself to feel the pain of the situation. For nine months, the country seemed possessed with the trial. My thoughts wandered. Why is America so obsessed with this trial? On the same day that Nicole Brown Simpson and Ronald Goldman were killed, a Hispanic man in San Jose had taken his gun and killed his wife, his children, and finally himself. This devastating event barely received mention in the newspapers.

I thought to myself that the O. J. trial is particularly difficult because of two very serious taboos for black men in America. The first taboo is to never become financially successful in America, and second, if you do, never, never marry a white person. Sex and race in America have a very peculiar history. Crossing the color line sexually had its limits. The most feared combination of the sexes seemed to be a black man marrying a white woman. This was forbidden. In the South, black women had always been available to white men, most times against their will. On the other hand, black men were demonized as relentless predators of white women, who were placed far above their reach. This was all too much to think about. The sexual history of African Americans and white Americans is grounded in fear, shame, and secrecy.

I had just seen the movie *Jefferson in Paris,* and I had been saddened by Jefferson's daughter's pain when she became aware of her father's affair with Sarah Hemsley, her mother's half sister. She spoke about the relationship between her father and Sarah, her father's slave, as being "unspeakable." These were issues that were not talked about.

As times have changed in our society, intermarriage has become more acceptable, but the fundamental emotional underpinnings are still present. This is an area where we as a society still need to do much emotional work. One of the reasons I had distanced myself from the trial was because I knew it would bring to the surface the forbidden issue of race and sex in a way that would be difficult to brush over. Knowing the American media, this was not likely to be particularly conducive to healing. I thought to myself that not only had O. J. married the forbidden fruit, he was now accused of murdering her. He would always live in infamy, even if he were to be acquitted. To make matters worse, every black man would pay for his alleged crimes. It does not seem possible for one black person to behave in a negative way without having that behavior attributed to all black people. There is a kind of collective guilt that most black people feel when one of us does something wrong or is accused of doing something wrong. When a crime occurs, we secretly pray that the suspect not be black, feeling that we will all have to suffer the collective condemnation.

I had never really thought much about O. J. Simpson being a role model for black people. In my mind, he was just another black football star who had become financially successful and used his finances to distance himself from his community and his heritage.

I thought back to my childhood, and the horrible race crimes I had heard about and witnessed. These crimes were committed *against* black people, in particular against black men, and no one was legally held accountable. Faceless and nameless men died just because they were black and in the wrong place at the wrong time. I recalled the rigid laws that existed in my very small town. It was known by everybody that if you were a black man and you happened to be walking on the sidewalk at the same time that a white woman was walking in your direction, you had to show respect by stepping off the walkway and casting your eyes in the opposite direction. You could not look at her or remain on the sidewalk as you walked past her.

One day a black man we all knew was hurriedly going to the local hardware store, and as he arrived at the store he barely noticed that he had walked past a white woman whom everybody knew. He did not get off the sidewalk, and she perceived him as looking at her, which she felt was totally disrespectful. That night, the man was tarred and feathered. This was a very common practice in Louisiana. To be tarred and feathered meant that you were beaten, bound, gagged, and dipped in hot tar and covered with feathers, then left to die. If you were lucky, you might be found before death overtook you, but in most cases, the treatment was fatal. Everyone was shocked and dismayed, but there was no one to report the crime to, because the very people who would have investigated the crime were also the perpetrators.

So O. J. had cast aside two very important taboos. He was successful, and he had married a white woman, and now he stood accused of murdering her. The trial would be "the trial of the century" not because it would aid us in healing ourselves but because it would raise the ugliness of racism as a powerful, divisive tool, and might very well succeed in dividing us all more deeply.

I felt great sadness as I was reminded of how deeply entrenched racism is in our country. Will we ever be able to move beyond our race-based beliefs? For the past ten years, I had been working on healing my personal attitudes and beliefs about race—focusing on how to move past form into content, learning to forgive, and learning that it was possible to choose peace instead of conflict and that love is the most powerful healing force in the world. This has been a struggle, because everything in our society has been defined by shapes, sizes, and color. Our kindergarten mentality keeps us divided, in fear and unable to align around what we have in common.

As I continued waiting for my plane, I shifted into my work mode, and started preparing for the workshop I was to give on Wednesday at this three-day, statewide mental health conference. I recalled my conversation with the mental health director who was responsible for my participation. She had been concerned about me using the word *healing* in the title of my workshop. She had suggested that I change the workshop name to make it more acceptable to the mental health professionals who would be attending the conference. I answered that I felt strongly that it was time for mental health professionals to learn to embrace the term *healing,* and see value in it for themselves as well as their clientele. After some discussion, we finally agreed to take a risk and leave the word *healing* in the title.

As I sat there in the airport terminal, I also thought more about Kentucky and wondered how I would resonate with the place and its people. Finally, I was able to board the plane, and off we went.

At last my plane landed in Louisville. I grabbed my luggage and proceeded on. I was met by a lovely man and his seven-year-old daughter. He took me directly to my hotel.

I woke up early on Tuesday and started my day with a meditation. I usually choose one of the twelve attitudinal healing principles to focus on throughout the day. I use it like a mantra, directly after my silent meditation. The principle for that day was "We can always perceive ourselves and others as either extending love or giving a call for help." Since I prefer to make the tenets as personal as possible, I recited to myself slowly: "I can always perceive myself and others as either extending love or giving a call for help." Kentucky is in the southeastern United States, with the southern tradition of "separate but equal," and I tend to associate it with prejudice and racism, even though I know from experience that this is not always the case. I was making a special point that morning to work on any tendency I might have to be judgmental of anything or anyone.

The first session I attended was very interesting. The focus was "Successful Advocacy," putting consumers and families first. Our lunch was to be a plenary session; the speaker's topic was "Maintaining a Value Base in a Managed Care Environment." This was an extremely important topic, since managed care was the biggest thing happening in the nation's health-care system and would impact the lives of many people dependent on the mental health system.

I went to lunch, and the room was filled to capacity. Apparently this was one of the largest conferences they had ever held. There were more than fifteen hundred professionals from all over the state of Kentucky. Although most of the seats were already taken, I found a perfect seat about seven tables away from the speaker's podium. The tables were huge, and there were already eleven people seated, receiving their salads. I asked the group if I could join them. Everyone was agreeable, and I sat down. As I introduced myself to each person, I observed to myself that everyone at the table was female.

As I waited for my salad, I noticed a huge screen on the stage, and I imagined that the speaker would be using it for the purposes of his presentation. I was finally served my salad and slowly began to eat as I engaged in some small talk with some of the women. I shared with them a bit about the program I work with in Oakland. The plenary session began, and everyone focused on the director of mental health. She began by announcing the speaker's name and topic. Next, she announced that the huge screen was up because at 1:00 P.M., which is 10 A.M. California time, they would be turning on the television so that everyone could view the O. J. verdict. At that moment, the keynote speaker for the lunch plenary lost his audience. I was appalled. I could not believe it. I immediately searched my memory bank for my mantra of the day: "I can always perceive myself and others as either extending love or giving a call for help." I was in the middle of eating my salad, in the heartland of America, at a statewide mental health conference, feeling trapped into listening to the O. J. verdict.

The keynote speaker stood up and began his lecture. He knew he had lost his audience. The background noise level in the room reflected a constant, low mumbling sound. I felt joined with the speaker, as his desperation became mine. I was focusing on listening to him. He began by appealing to the professionals present not to allow managed care and the diminishing dollar to decrease the level of care to their clients.

His passion, however, could not match the fervor and zeal of the emotions felt by the audience for the O. J. verdict. At my table, the women were taking bets. One very outspoken woman, a leader in her profession, was holding the bets for everyone. I was attempting to ignore them as I stared relentlessly at the speaker. I was determined to give him my attention. I listened even more intently, trying to hang on to his words. The speaker was passionate about his topic, and was not going to submit to losing his already-lost audience.

Then I heard someone ask me, "How will you bet? Guilty or innocent?" I sat there stunned, unable to respond to her request. Again the words came into my hearing range: "How will you bet? Guilty or innocent?" I looked at her meekly and replied, "I do not bet." She looked back at me and said without blinking an eye, "One neutral." I wanted to respond, but I felt it would take away from the speaker, so I quickly put my attention back on him.

The situation continued to worsen, and the speaker's microphone went out. As some attendees tried to fix the microphone, I could see that the speaker was determined not to give up. With no microphone, he continued to speak, while the noise level went up about twenty decibels. No one was listening to him! Again, my heart felt joined with his. I was determined to listen to his talk even though I could not hear a word he was saying.

The women at my table were busy discussing the pending verdict. I felt lost! I could not hear the speaker, and I was not interested in the O. J. verdict. I looked around the room. Everyone was busy discussing the "trial of the century." The speaker was desperately completing his talk, and I was wondering how we as health-care professionals were going to manage our care when we could not even listen to a lecture on managed care. I clearly experienced a call for help.

The speaker finally finished his talk and sat down. No one seemed to notice that he had finished because they were not listening. One o'clock arrived, and the television was turned on, CNN, live from Los Angeles. The huge room filled with mental health professionals came to a standstill. Everyone was totally quiet at last, intently focused on the television. For the first time, the audience was silent and poised for listening. I thought back on the speaker and how he had competed for attention and had not received it. I listened, and I heard more than the verdict. I heard the heartbeat of a nation. The heartbeat of the world. I was deep in thought when the verdict came: "Not Guilty" echoed throughout the room. In a moment, the emotions of anger and rage flooded the room. Had the emotions been blood, the floor would have been covered with it. I began to wonder why I was in Kentucky at a statewide mental health conference during this time.

Suddenly, a stern voice rang out across the table. "How would you have bet?" I was deep in thought. For the first time, I was noticing that I was the only black person at the table, and one of only about ten at the entire conference. Again I heard the woman's voice from across the table, asking me in a very firm tone, "How would you have bet?" I was unsure what to say, so I decided to be honest. I replied in no uncertain terms that I had been in a state of recovery ever since June of 1994, when O. J. had not committed suicide. Of course, had he not been a very famous football star, he would have been a very dead human being; as soon as the chase began, they would have shot him, and there wouldn't have been any story. Everyone at the table began to stare at me. "I personally did not want to go through this process," I told them. "When I first heard about O. J. being charged with the murders, I knew that we—the American public—would be in for an emotional roller coaster. I knew how infected we all are with racism and the other 'isms,' and I just did not want to go through it. I knew that my desire was totally selfish. *I just don't think we are willing yet to be healed.* However, now having witnessed our behavior in the ensuing year and a half, I realize that O. J. could not commit suicide, because if he had, we would not have had this opportunity to see ourselves. The trial provided a mirror for us. Certainly the color division revealed by our reactions is a wake-up call for all of us. We have been given the gift of seeing and feeling just how infected we are with the disease of racism. Now we must look deeply into our hearts and ask ourselves: Are we willing to be healed?"

As I listened to myself say these words, I became fully aware of the women sitting at the table with me. For the first time, they were truly seeing me, and I them. One of the women spoke up, saying she was very sad about the entire process.

She had tears in her eyes as she spoke of her pain and shame. Right there in that lunch room, we were experiencing a Healing Racism Circle. This woman spoke of how she had been hypnotized by the trial and found herself addicted to it daily. Another woman chimed in, saying that she had become aware of her racial feelings as a result of the trial, and she didn't know what to do with them. We all sat there in that huge room, unable to move. We had awakened to the pain of our race-based beliefs. I was now aware of why I was in Kentucky at that moment and grateful for the tenet "I can always perceive myself and others as either extending love or giving a call for help."

As I write this well over two years have passed, and Americans have become noticeably bored with the O. J. trials, including the civil verdict awarding millions of dollars in compensatory damages to the families of Nicole Brown Simpson and Ronald Goldman. In the second trial, the mostly white jurors found O. J. responsible. Again I was saddened, because of the emotional state of our society reflected by the coverage and reactions to both trials. While the judge in the second trial was more skillful in keeping the issue of race to a minimum, it was still the ground of being that provided the context. Remarks such as those recorded in the *Oakland Tribune*, in which a white lawyer remarked, "I think we have twelve intelligent jurors who have made a decision and I think that justice has prevailed finally" and "I think this jury was more intelligent and unbiased," still reflect the deep chasm that divides us.

In reading and hearing all the race issues that surfaced during the two trials, I am more than ever convinced that we must do the heart work necessary to heal the pain and venom of racism. I don't think that any of us were left unscarred during this trial. The polarization that was caused by the verdicts can happen again and again in America because we haven't yet healed the underlying conditions that breed racism. America has wished and hoped racism would go away, but this only keeps us caught in an endless mad dream.

The shift made palpable at that luncheon table in Kentucky, when we women opened our hearts to each other and talked about our honest reactions, illustrates the kinds of risks necessary if we are to find healing. The women at the table were not trying to hurt me or be insensitive. Once I saw them as asking for love, this opened the door to their being able to begin to hear me and sense my pain as they shared their own. This is what is meant by the attitudinal healing principle: "We can always perceive ourselves and others as either extending love or giving a call for help."

It is through this individual heart work that we will begin to realize the message conveyed in Martin Luther King, Jr.'s words: "This is our hope. This is the faith that I go back to the South with. With this faith we will be able to hew out of the mountain of despair, a stone of hope. With this faith, we will be able to transform the jangling discords of our nation into a beautiful symphony of brotherhood [and sisterhood]."

Changing Our Perceptions

The challenge we face with the final attitudinal healing principle is developing the discernment and ability to recognize when others are giving a call for help or extending love, even when the appearances seem quite the contrary. Our capacity to perceive in this way creates a readiness for healing that triggers right action. It allows us to release or to be released from our pain and our fear.

Many times, it is not immediately obvious when a call for help is being given. For example, when I (Aeeshah) was invited by the woman at the Kentucky conference to place a bet on the day of the infamous O. J. verdict, I refused to bet. After the verdict one of the women wanted to know how I would have bet. Her question was a call for help, but I could very well have experienced this as an attack. It is our willingness to heal that motivates our ability to see and take advantage of these subtle opportunities for healing.

Another opportunity for healing arises on those occasions when people open their hearts to one another and talk honestly about their fears. If we truly desire racial healing, we are called upon to take the risk and be vulnerable. This risk taking opens the doors for extending love as well as seeing and answering the call for help. When a person extends love, the message can be felt by all who are near. We then become one with the statement from *A Course in Miracles:* "My brother's [and sister's] pain and my pain are the same." This concept is eloquently echoed by Ralph Waldo Emerson: "The only way to have a friend is to be one."

PUTTING PRINCIPLE #12 INTO PRACTICE

"We can always perceive ourselves and others as either extending love or giving a call for help."

1. Write about two or three characteristics about yourself that demonstrate your ability to extend love to someone whom you perceive as different from yourself.

2. Bring to mind any occasion that you have experienced in which you answered a call for help from the

"other." If you cannot remember such an incident, imagine what one might be like.

3. Write about any time in which you experienced an intimate interaction with someone from another race.

4. Take a moment to look into your past. Have you on any occasion been in a situation in which you felt you were being attacked by a member of another race and made a choice to see that situation differently? How were you able to see differently? What was the most important factor in helping you shift from fear to love in that situation? If you weren't able to make the shift and stayed caught in fear, imagine how you might be able to choose love now that your understanding is deepening.

CHAPTER SIXTEEN

A New Beginning: Healing Racism Circles

To declare with unfaltering voice
The Unity of God, the Brotherhood [and Sisterhood] of [humanity],
And Grace and Mercy, Bounty and Love,
Poured out in unstinted measure for ever and ever.

THE HOLY QURAN

As we approach the task of racial healing, we are called upon to do the heart work of looking at our prejudices, our biases, and our misperceptions. To do this, we must ask for help, because to look at these areas alone can be so painful that we may not persevere. Our goal is healing, not to get stuck in our painful past. Two of our dearest friends, Diane Cirincione and Jerry Jampolsky, shared with us the following truth: "Forgiveness is giving up all hope of a better past." The challenge is accepting a new beginning in which we willingly let go of everything that gets in the way of our goal of experiencing inner peace grounded in unconditional love. This will require practice, because this way of seeing is new and involves looking on your world without fear and judgment and with forgiveness and love. We hope our stories have helped you understand what we have done to work on ourselves. That work is ongoing. Each day we pray this prayer for humanity:

A New Beginning: Healing Racism Circles

From the North to the South
From the East to the West
To the Spirit of light among us
And the Spirits below
May all beings be serene
May all beings be happy
May all beings be at peace

ANDREW DA PASANO
Founder of the Temple of Esoteric Sciences

Let us remember that this new beginning is continuous. Let us always exercise the willingness to ask for help when we experience a need to condemn or judge our fellow human beings for their shortcomings. Let us remember always these words from *A Course in Miracles:* "The answer that I give my brother [sister] is what I am asking for. And what I learn of him [her] is what I learn about myself."

Healing racism requires an intensely personal decision, but once we make the choice for healing, helpers come from all walks of life to usher us closer to our goal of healing. So don't be afraid to ask to see differently, because only then can true learning begin.

Healing Racism Circles

At our Attitudinal Healing Connection (AHC) center in West Oakland, we assemble groups as part of the Healing Racism Project. Our mission is to teach that ignorance is the ancestor of fear, and healing is letting go of fear.

This group process was developed by us to create classrooms in which people are safe to do the personal and spiritual work that will heal the racial wounds of prejudice and bigotry. A recipient of the Jerry Jampolsky Award for Excellence, the Healing Racism Project is now internationally recognized for its work in racism.

The Attitudinal Healing Connection grew out of a group of diverse individuals seeking to heal themselves through joining together. We wanted to heal ourselves of our prejudices and fears about the "other" and also to teach what we learned. We define racism, both institutionalized and internalized, as a life-threatening illness that causes pain and anguish and is passed on from generation to generation. Our attempt is to encourage people of every race to explore their negative beliefs about the "other" and to ask for spiritual help in letting go of these beliefs.

To help us, we meet as a group and utilize the age-old spiritual processes of ritual, drumming, and storytelling as means of releasing feelings of guilt, judgment, fear, and shame in a safe and nonthreatening way. We create a new village called the Drum Tribe. All who participate make a decision to do the work that will heal these issues personally. Our hope is that each of us will develop the willingness to look at this issue, acknowledge our feelings, thoughts, and beliefs about race and racism, and begin to learn to see differently. Our primary goal is to create a safe place where we can begin to explore and bring our unconscious racial fears to the surface so we can understand and release them.

As individuals, we find a meeting of hearts and minds as we join in this process and bring up our unconscious beliefs about who we are as human beings. We expand in our ability to foster communication not only across racial and ethnic lines, but also within our own hearts and minds. All the work we're talking about is inner work first, then role modeling within our Drum Tribe. As we recognize our underlying unity, we can then make a difference and make changes in the larger world.

At a recent group meeting, ten people sat in a small circle, drumming in unison to unite their energy. Seven of the people in the room were black, three were white. Two were grandparents, and a few were gay. All knew what it is like to experience some form of prejudice. As the drumming ceased, we read the twelve principles of attitudinal healing just described. For the following two hours, these ten people shared their personal experiences with racism, asking only to be listened to within the circle of safety, validation, and acceptance.

Everyone is affected by the disease of racism. It eats at the hearts and minds of every human being. Rodney King asked, "Why can't we all just get along?" As we enter the dawn of a new millennium, we're still wondering uncomfortably how to deal with this challenging issue. Many of us watched the O. J. Simpson criminal and civil trials and immediately became polarized when the verdicts were announced. We seem unable to avoid judging the Million Man March or the Million Woman March. The violent racial flare-ups in inner city communities, schools, and prisons further validate the fact that we can no longer deny the issue of race. The times we live in urge us to uncover, explore, and heal the pain that we have inflicted on one another.

Recently, we had the opportunity to present a seminar at the fall staff conference for the University of California at Davis. During the group dialogue, one woman of Japanese descent shared an experience that was very difficult for her. She had been living in Davis, California, since she was a young woman and had raised her children there. She had considered herself to be liberal and was supportive of equal rights for all. It was not until her daughter went off to Los Angeles to attend the University of California campus there that she began to learn more about her own prejudices.

While away at college, her daughter began to date a young man of a different race. When her daughter called to tell her that she was in love with a young black man and wanted to bring him home, she was quite alarmed. The whole idea made her very unhappy, and she felt she could not accept it. She was forced to look her prejudice squarely in the face, and she felt great pain and fear around the issue.

Even though she had easily called herself liberal and had felt that she was without prejudice, when it came to her family— especially her children—her deeper feelings had surfaced. She admitted that she did not want to continue the cycle of rejection and pain, and she did not want to alienate her daughter. She picked up a card with the twelve principles of attitudinal healing printed on it and spoke of wanting to use these principles to help her see her potential son-in-law differently.

We shared with this woman our belief that this is the work we all have to do, and that we were sure that if she continued to be open and share her desire to heal, others would join her. For this is our experience: When we listen empathically to another human being, when we listen deeply and are truly present without judgment, our hearts become joined. Something happens when a human being is talking to you and you listen empathically. Something takes place between you, which creates a deep respect and even a bond between you. This happens even if you don't agree with everything the person is saying; by listening deeply, you go beneath the level of opinion and bond on a heart level.

Attitudinal healing itself is a process of changing our perceptions about someone or some situation from a state of fear to a state of love. The first principle of attitudinal healing reads: "The essence of our being is love." This tenet is the foundation of the work that we do in our classrooms for racial healing. By encouraging empowerment through the attitudinal healing principles, we emphasize that we always have choices, and that we can choose peace instead of conflict. The ability to choose is one of the most powerful tools humanity has for change. Hopelessness and powerlessness always decrease whenever one individual chooses to see differently. Each person can make a difference. We believe that through dialogue in nonjudgmental, safe group environments, we can make the best progress toward this goal. As we begin to heal, we will begin to rebuild our community, and in rebuilding our communities, we will be rebuilding the family. Racism has done so much to destroy the true inner human being, and healing racism is all about reconnecting and rebuilding the inner human being and reaffirming our purpose in life here on earth.

Forming Healing Racism Circles

Healing Racism Circles provide one of the best settings we know of for opening the door to healing the wounds of racism. We would like to see this idea spread across the country and be implemented in every city and town.

We encourage you to consider forming a Healing Racism Circle where you live. You might invite family members, co-workers, friends, or neighbors to attend. You could advertise in local community newspapers to find others who are interested. The following basic principles will give you some ideas on how to structure your group. Please feel free to contact us (see the section on Resources at the back of the book) if you need assistance in getting started.

Basic Principles in Holding
a Healing Racism Circle

We start each Healing Racism Circle with group drumming to help us come together in unity on the deepest level. Then we read together the following principles of agreement.

1. Recognizing that the essence of each of us is love, we agree to honor and respect one another. We recognize that each of us is of equal value.
2. We are here together to learn about the disease of racism and to promote as well as experience a personal healing process.
3. We recognize that love is listening, and we agree to listen with an open heart, to give mutual support, and to practice nonjudgmental listening and sharing.
4. We realize that when we love and have compassion for ourselves, then we're able to extend that same love and compassion to others.
5. We are here to heal ourselves, not to give advice or to change anyone's beliefs or behavior.
6. We share from our own experience by risking and exposing our own emotional state; in this way, we find common experience for joining.
7. We respect ourselves and each other as unique, and we recognize that each person's process is important, not our judgment of it.
8. The roles of student and teachers are interchangeable, and they fluctuate from one to the other regardless of age or experience.
9. We agree that we have a common goal of inner peace, and that it is from that place of peace that we come

together to find the best answers for the work we are
carrying out.

10. We are willing to risk exposing our feelings openly and
honestly without attacking others in order to create a
space where clear communication is supported and
joining can be experienced.

11. We agree to keep in mind that we always have a choice
between peace and conflict, between love and fear.

12. We agree to confidentiality regarding what we share in
this circle; what is said during this very sensitive process
must stay among the participants.

Ten Things You Can Do to Help Heal Racism

We would like to leave you with some practical things you
can do on a day-to-day level to help heal racism. If everyone
who reads this books puts into practice even one of these ten
things, the world will change.

1. I will do my best to put into practice in my daily life the
twelve attitudinal healing principles.

2. I commit myself to speaking up when I hear someone
making a racist remark, while endeavoring to see this as
a call for help, and coming from a place of compassion.

3. I commit myself to learning more about cultures and
ethnic groups that I consider to be the "other."

4. I will work to understand that admitting that racism is a
problem is the first step that I can take toward recovery
and healing.

5. I will strive to be open-minded by practicing the art
of nonjudgmental acceptance of racial and ethnic
differences.

6. I believe that who I am and what I believe are valuable; therefore, I know I can make a difference, and I intend to do my part to bridge the gap of the racial divide.
7. Each day, I intend to honor and accept differences.
8. I recognize that racism is based on power and is embedded institutionally. I will do my part to encourage institutions to embrace the concept of racial healing.
9. I am willing to acknowledge attitudes and beliefs I am holding that are based in racial prejudice and bigotry.
10. I will hold in my heart the belief that love is the answer to any issue I may encounter that is grounded in fear and racial prejudice, whether it is with myself or someone else.

Throughout this book, we have endeavored to share with you the experiences and exercises that we have put into practice to heal ourselves, but we realize that for these practical guides to be effective, each of us must do the work as an individual, in our own unique way. We hope that you will modify the experiences and exercises to increase your personal healing around this extremely challenging issue. Racism has many layers, and the healing process can be arduous. We have worked personally for many years to heal from this disease, and we hope our experiences will make it a little easier for you as you embark on your own path to healing.

How are we to build a new humanity? Only by leading
[human beings] toward a true, inalienable ethic of our own,
which is capable of further development. But this goal cannot be
reached unless countless individuals will transform themselves
from blind [people] into seeing ones and begin to spell out the
great commandment, which is: Reverence for Life.

ALBERT SCHWEITZER

Epilogue

Without the rich heart, wealth is an ugly beggar.

RALPH WALDO EMERSON

As we shared our stories and the times we were able to overcome our challenges, we asked that all would be forgiven and released from the illusions of separation along with us. We know that race categorizations do not really exist. We made them up. There is really no such thing as different races. There is only one race—the human race.

Nevertheless, racism or fear of the "other" is one of the most painful issues confronting America and the world today. We know that there are no quick fixes, but through consistent, honest, heartfelt dialogue, we can reach a place of peace with this issue. We know that the roots of racism lie in fear and greed. We have defined racism as a life-threatening illness that we are all dying from. We believe that we can relieve ourselves of this malady by taking personal responsibility for our own healing process.

We believe that when we are healed as individuals, we are never healed alone. Therefore, we include all in our personal healing process. A cornerstone of our beliefs is that we are not here to change other people. We hope that as you journeyed with us through this book, you were able to be one with us in the process. We believe that as long as one human being is bound and shackled, we are all bound and shackled. We believe that if we clean up our minds about the "other," we can do much to eliminate pollution on the planet. Our negative thoughts about ourselves and others add more pollution to the planet than any chemical plant.

Earlier we quoted from Lao-tzu: "The wholeness of life has, from of old, been made manifest in its parts." We wear this metaphor as a badge of honor to remind us to look on the whole of life rather than the fragments. As we truly embrace the belief that the essence of our being is love, we include all of us as part of that essence.

Let us assist one another in becoming love finders rather than fault finders. As the Bible says: Seek and ye shall find. We can learn to love ourselves and all beings by forgiving rather than judging. Let us awaken to the understanding that perception is a mirror, not reality, and in any situation we can always perceive ourselves and others as either extending love or giving a call for help.

We are deeply aware that the road to racial healing requires us to be like the Sankofa bird, the symbol from the Akan Tribe of Ghana, West Africa, which we mentioned earlier. Like the Sankofa bird, in order to move forward we must reach back to cleanse our past, so that we can then move harmoniously forward. Let us not be afraid to explore the past. Looking at the past through the eyes of forgiveness is one way we can stop the pain, fear, and guilt of our painful collective history from destroying the present.

Each day as we embrace the sun with love and joy, we can come to the realization that giving and receiving are the same. Therefore, we will give equally without reservation of affection and prayer. Let us affirm that the past can no longer hurt us and that we are too occupied with the present to worry about the future. This instant is the only time there is. Let us make oneness (*ekome*) our single goal.

Epilogue

I desire this Holy Instant for myself, that I may share it
with my brother [and sister], whom I love.

It is not possible that I can have it without him [her] or he [she]
without me. Yet it is wholly possible for us to share it now.

And so I choose this instant as the one to offer to the Holy Spirit,
that [the Holy Spirit's] blessing may descend on us,
and keep us both in peace.

A COURSE IN MIRACLES

Resources

Attitudinal Healing Centers

Attitudinal Healing
Connection, Inc.
P.O. Box 2350
Oakland, CA 94623
510-652-5530
Fax: 510-652-8233
E-mail: healco@aol.com

The Network for Attitudinal
Healing International
P.O. Box 390129
Kailua-Kona, HI 96739
888-222-7205
Fax: 808-322-8894
E-mail: NetAttHeal@aol.com

Healing Racism Workshops, Lectures, and Talks

Aeeshah Ababio Clottey
and Kokomon Clottey
Attitudinal Healing
Connection, Inc.
P.O. Box 2350
Oakland, CA 94623
510-652-5530
Fax: 510-652-8233
E-mail: healco@aol.com

Healing the Heart of
Diversity
Patricia Moore Harbour,
Director
John E. Fetzer Institute
9292 West KL Avenue
Kalamazoo, MI 49009-9398

Healing Racism Institute
Charles Young
P.O. Box 110
Evanston, IL 60204
708-492-0123

Dr. Tom Pinkson
Wakan Community
240 Miller Avenue
Mill Valley, CA 94941
415-381-3909

The National Conference
Orange County Chapter
5000 Birch Street,
  Suite 2900
Newport Beach, CA 92660
714-668-9191

Iris Films
(Distributes the films
  Skin Deep and
  Talking About Race)
2600 Tenth Street, Suite 413
Berkeley, CA 94710

Stir-Fry Seminars
Lee Mun Wah
(Distributes the film
  The Color of Fear)
470 Third Street
Oakland, CA 94607
510-419-3930 or
  800-370-STIR

Coastal Carolina University
(Distributes the films *Calling
  All Colors* and *The Quilts*)
Center for Education and
  Community
P.O. Box 261954
Conway, SC 29528
803-349-2672

Finding Out About *A Course in Miracles*

The Miracle Distribution Center
(Distributes materials related to *A Course in Miracles*)
1141 E. Ash Avenue
Fullerton, CA 92631
714-738-8380

About the Authors

Aeeshah Ababio Clottey

Aeeshah Ababio is the founder and executive director of the Attitudinal Healing Connection, Inc., in Oakland California. Our mission is to teach that ignorance is the ancestor of fear, and healing is letting go of fear. Our goal is to provide alternative treatment modalities that will aid in the shift in perception from fear to love in a community. Aeeshah focuses on racial healing for the professional and lay communities via a variety of workshops, trainings, and support groups.

For seventeen years, Aeeshah has worked on specialized training in attitudinal healing under the guidance and support of Dr. Gerald (Jerry) Jampolsky of Tiburon, California, the author of many books on the subject and the founder of the first Center for Attitudinal Healing. Aeeshah received her formal education at the University of California at Berkeley. She is also a California State Certified Genetic Counselor.

Aeeshah is a consultant at the Center for Attitudinal Healing in Tiburon and the assistant program director at Casa de la Vida, a residential treatment center in Oakland, where she utilizes attitudinal healing concepts as a ground of being for effectively working with consumers in the mental health system.

Aeeshah is internationally recognized for her work in healing racism. In 1993, she received the Jerry Jampolsky Award for excellence for the Healing Racism Project, made possible by the John Fetzer Institute.

Aeeshah may be contacted at the Attitudinal Healing Connection, Inc., 3278 West Street, Oakland, CA 94608; 510-652-5530; E-mail: healco@aol.com.

Kokomon Clottey

Kokomon Clottey was born to the Ga-Adagbe Tribe in Accra, the capital of Ghana in West Africa. The Ga society is rich with ancient codes of conduct, deep spiritual beliefs, and awesome rituals of power. Kokomon is a medicine man and interpreter of this ancient African tribe's wisdom and rituals. It was the local master of the drummers of the Ga Tribe who gave him the foundation for his drumming skills.

Kokomon moved to the United States in 1977. He brings to the stage thirty years of performing experience and musical training from the Royal Schools of Music Workshop in London as well as the Dick Grove School of Music.

Kokomon is a many-faceted man capable of painting rainbows in the sky. He is a storyteller, record producer, author, and teacher. He composed and produced the *Gifts of God* audio-cassette.

Kokomon is the cofounder of the Attitudinal Healing Connection, Inc., in Oakland California, an organization that is internationally recognized for its work in racial healing. He is also cofounder of the Center for Attitudinal Healing in Ghana, West Africa.

Kokomon has just produced his first compact disk, *Love Is the Answer*, released in the fall of 1997, and is the coauthor with his wife Aeeshah of *Beyond Fear: Twelve Spiritual Keys to Racial Healing.*

Kokomon may be contacted at the Attitudinal Healing Connection, Inc., 3278 West Street, Oakland, CA 94608; 510-652-5530; E-mail: healco@aol.com.

Attitudinal Healing Connection, Inc.

We appreciate your interest in the work of Attitudinal Healing Connection, Inc. The Attitudinal Healing Connection is dedicated to bringing people to the realization that ignorance is the ancestor of fear, and healing is letting go of fear. We have real solutions in the areas of race relations, early childhood violence prevention, and promoting self-sufficiency in Africa. We are a nonprofit organization based in Oakland, California, with a sister organization in Ghana, West Africa. You may donate your cash or your appreciated securities and avoid payment of capital gains tax on your gift. We need your support so we can grow in California and Africa.

For further information and to learn specifics about the programs and workshops listed below, contact:

The Attitudinal Healing Connection, Inc.
3278 West Street
Oakland, CA 94608
E-mail: healco@aol.com
510-652-5530
Fax: 510-652-8233

Attitudinal Healing Programs Offered

Person to Person: Nonjudgmental support group for individuals and families in crisis.

Healing Racism Circle: Focus: To engage in deep dialogue that allows for authentic communication.

Art-Esteem for Children: Creates an avenue for children to tell their stories through artistic mediums. Focus: Early childhood violence prevention.

After-School Mentoring: Support group for children to assist them in their schoolwork and offer unconditional love. Focus: Violence prevention.

School Outreach: Storytelling and African drumming via school assemblies. Focus: Youth learning and understanding the power of choice.

Ghana Project: Support our Sister Center in Africa to integrate the essence of sufficiency with the principles of attitudinal healing.

Healing Racism Project

At the Attitudinal Healing Connection, we feel strongly that institutionalized and internalized racism is a life-threatening illness in our society. Through workshops, trainings, and conferences, this project applies the principles and processes of attitudinal healing to the issues of ethnic tension and racial conflict. In the workshops we explore attitudes and beliefs about cultural and ethnic differences; engage in deep dialogue that allows authentic communication; harmonize emotions through ritual and African drumming; and transcend the hopeless cycle of "attack and defense" by doing the work of forgiveness.

ALSO FROM H J KRAMER

FULL ESTEEM AHEAD:
100 Ways to Build Self-Esteem in Children and Adults
by Diane Loomans with Julia Loomans
"*Full Esteem Ahead* is the best book on parenting and self-esteem
that I know."—Jack Canfield, author of *Chicken Soup for the Soul*

RECLAIMING OUR HEALTH:
Exploding the Medical Myth and Embracing
the Source of True Healing
by John Robbins
In his rousing and inspiring style, John Robbins, author of *Diet
for a New America*, turns his attention to the national debate on
health care.

WAY OF THE PEACEFUL WARRIOR:
A Book That Changes Lives
by Dan Millman
A spiritual classic! The international best-seller that speaks
directly to the universal quest for happiness.

THE LAST OF THE DREAM PEOPLE
by Alice Anne Parker
At once a hauntingly erotic love story and a gripping tale of
adventure set in Southeast Asia during World War II, *The Last
of the Dream People* skillfully explores the mysterious realms
between waking and dreaming, life and death.

THE LIFE YOU WERE BORN TO LIVE:
A Guide to Finding Your Life Purpose
by Dan Millman
Dan Millman's popular Life-Purpose System features key
spiritual laws to help understand your past, clarify your present,
and change your future.

If you are unable to find these books in your favorite bookstore,
please call 800-833-9327.

For a free book catalog, please send your name and address to
H J Kramer, P.O. Box 1082, Tiburon, CA 94920.